Fly Fishing

in Rivers and Streams

The Techniques and Tactics of Streamcraft

Fly Fishing
in Rivers and Streams

The Techniques and Tactics of Streamcraft

Terry Lawton

Ragged Mountain Press / McGraw-Hill
Camden, Maine ▮ New York ▮
Chicago ▮ San Francisco ▮ Lisbon ▮ London ▮
Madrid ▮ Mexico City ▮
Milan ▮ New Delhi ▮ San Juan ▮ Seoul ▮ Singapore
▮ Sydney ▮ Toronto

The McGraw·Hill Companies

1 2 3 4 5 6 7 8 9 IMP IMP 9 8 7
Published by Ragged Mountain Press/McGraw-Hill
www.raggedmountainpress.com

First published in 2007 by New Holland Publishers Ltd

Printed and bound in Singapore.

ISBN-13: 978-0-07-149433-5
ISBN-10: 0-07-1-149433-2

Library of Congress Cataloging-in-Publication Data is available.

Questions regarding the content of this book should be addressed to
Ragged Mountain Press
P.O. Box 220
Camden, ME 04843

Questions regarding the ordering of this book should be addressed to
The McGraw-Hill Companies
Customer Service Department
P.O. Box 547
Blacklick, OH 43004
Retail customers: 1-800-262-4729
Bookstores: 1-800-722-4726

Cover photography by Terry Lawton
Title page: Miekak, in Swedish Lapland, is a great place to fish for Arctic char.
Opposite: The Madison River, Montana.
Pages 6-7: A trout rises on the East Gallatin River, Montana.

CONTENTS

INTRODUCTION

Newcomers to fly fishing who may have started to learn to fly fish by attending a seminar, or having some casting lessons, and those who haven't had the benefit of an experienced friend to 'show them the ropes', can spend a lot of time spooking fish. Eventually, we hope, they start hooking fish, but they also probably start losing them because they lack knowledge of the real practicalities of fly fishing. What they need is streamcraft. I hope this book will be of interest and practical benefit to new anglers as well as the more experienced ones who are looking for guidance on streamcraft and a more thoughtful approach to fishing different rivers and streams. Anyone can take casting lessons and get someone to show them how to catch a fish every now and then, but to really succeed as a fly fisherman you need to learn so much more. This book will not tell you how to cast (I make no pretence at being a casting instructor, and there are some very good books, videos and DVDs available, as well as an increasing number of qualified instructors), but it will help you to understand what you are trying to do, and also to catch more fish.

Fly fishing does have an ability to appear unnecessarily complicated, and some anglers revel in this complexity. They may continually change lines and leaders to match changing conditions on the water, for example. For others who stick to the same rod, line and leader from one season to the next, such complexity is anathema, but when the same old tactics, tackle and flies stop working, then you will have to make changes and try something different. But what exactly should you change? A good place to start making changes is your fly – either to a different size or a different pattern. To be able to make changes quickly is a big help, and it's worth practicing tying knots at home so that you can tie them quickly and properly on the river bank. Be sure to always stow your fly boxes in the same pocket, so that you know where they are. This can save valuable time.

As anglers gain more experience, they tend to approach their fishing in different ways according to their character. Some of them are quite happy to sit, watch, wait for a rise, make a cast or two and catch the fish before moving on to look for another one. I know a man who does this very successfully, sitting and smoking his pipe while he waits. Others like to keep busy – I count myself in this group – casting to likely lies if fish are not showing, and probably not spending as much time as they should observing. Whichever approach you have, you need to come to terms with many variables, the importance of which change according to the river, the season and even the time of day. As each variable changes, so it affects all the other variables.

Fly fishing can be a frustrating sport: One day you can catch a bonanza of fish, but the next day the fish won't so much as look at your fly. It is this dynamic – and the challenge to find what tactics and flies will work – that makes fly-fishing so rewarding. To find a day when conditions are such that catching fish is difficult enough to make it challenging, but you can catch enough to make the day rewarding, is not easy, but such days do happen. I hope that when you have finished reading this book, what you have discovered may help you to turn some of those impossible days into really rewarding occasions.

I have arranged the contents of this book into what I consider to be a logical order. You cannot cast a fly or catch a fish without a suitable rod, reel and line. If you are a complete beginner, these are the first things that you will buy. If you are an experienced angler, you may be looking to buy a new and better rod or line. You need the equipment that is best suited to the type of fishing that occupies most of your time.

One of the great delights of fishing is that there are so many items of equipment and accessories on the market, but to some people this is a nightmare. For them, I have tried to limit my discussion to a list of essential items. If, however, you are an ardent tackle collector and gadget-monger, by all means go and buy that latest 'must have' gizmo, but don't be surprised if you never use it or you discard it quickly.

The chapter on wading is much as the title suggests: it's all about wading and – perhaps just as important – not wading. In this chapter we'll take a look at the equipment, the techniques and the question of safety when in the water.

Choosing flies and whether or not to match the hatch is an argument – and a philosophy – that continues to run and run. Maybe I am treading on dangerous ground by even entering into it, but it's an important debate.

Now we come to the essence of this book. For me, streamcraft is what so much of fishing is about. Whether you like it or not, humans are hunters, and hunting skills are not very far below the surface of even the most urban persons today. If you can look at a piece of water and work out for yourself where fish are likely to be found, approach within casting distance without frightening them, present a fly and catch a fish, then you are well on the way to becoming an angler and not just someone who can catch only the easy fish in a heavily stocked water.

When everything goes right and you catch a fish, then you need to know how to play it and bring it to hand so that you can either release it to grow bigger or, if you want to take a fish home to eat for supper, kill it quickly and humanely. Whatever you do with the fish that you catch, do treat them with respect, dispatching them quickly or releasing them back to the river with the minimum of trauma and fuss.

Your fellow anglers deserve respect, too, so treat them in the same way that you would have them treat you. Sadly, not everyone abides by this simple code.

Sooner or later you will want to fish some of the big name rivers across North America, if you have not done so already. Probably one of the most important factors when embarking upon such an adventure is to treat a fishing trip with an open mind. The rivers and streams encountered will be different from those at home, and you may be forced to use different techniques, which is, of course, one of the best things about fishing in new waters.

No book on fly fishing would be complete without recommending some essential flies. The selection given in this book will enable most anglers to stand a chance of catching fish in many different rivers and streams. This selection may not be yours or your fishing partner's, but it will save the day for many.

And finally, if you can't tie a limited selection of knots competently and consistently, don't expect to land any fish that you catch.

Besides its practical elements, within this book I have also tried to capture the soul, spirit and atmosphere of fly fishing. I think that these are equally important aspects of angling. Yes, we all want to catch fish, but there is – or should be – genuinely more to fishing than simply catching ever more fish. Everyone should enjoy their fishing. So let's get on to the water and start thinking about fly fishing.

Below: While we all want to catch fish when we go fishing, there is – or should be – genuinely more to fishing than catching large quantities of fish. Anglers should enjoy the act of fishing, as well as developing their skills and techniques on the water.

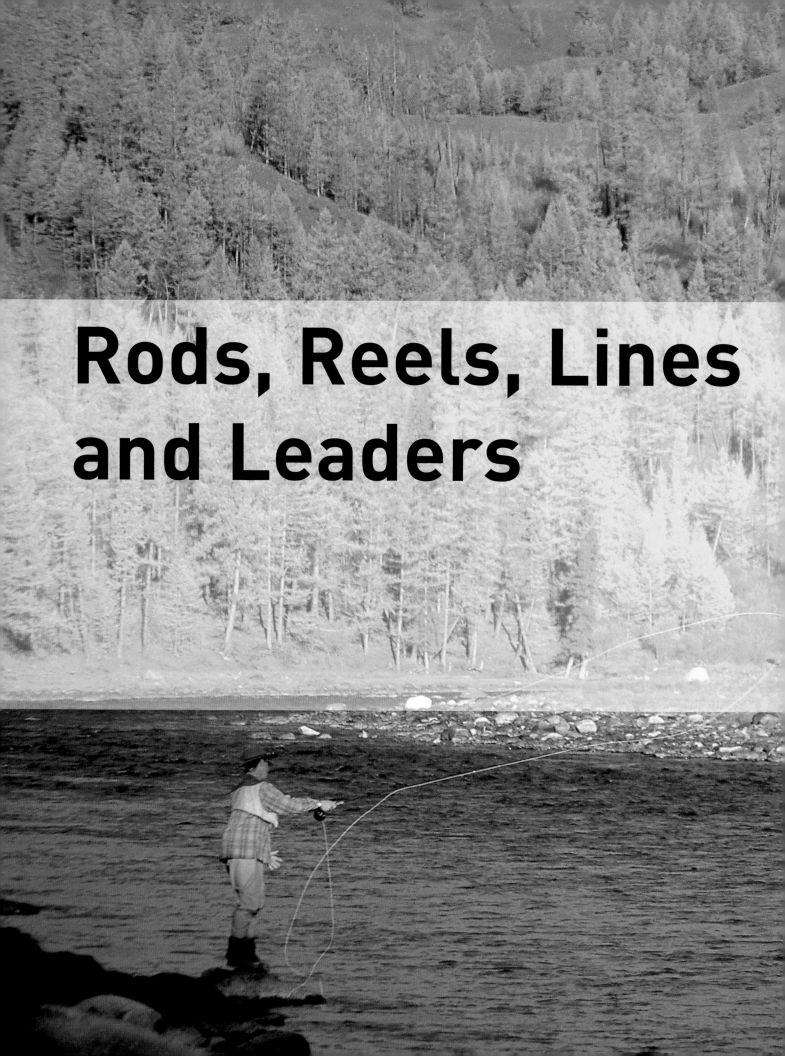

Rods, Reels, Lines and Leaders

Rods, Reels, Lines and Leaders

Fly fishing is so much more enjoyable when you're using tackle and equipment that you understand, and in which you have confidence. Fishing with a rod and line that you like using, that works for you and with you, and that is matched to your type of fishing will have a major effect on how successfully you fish and how much pleasure you take from your days on the river. Selecting the right tackle takes thought and research, but does not necessarily entail spending a lot of money.

To be able to fish successfully anywhere, you need to have confidence not only in your ability, but also in the tackle that you are using and in the fly on the end of your leader. Once you have put together an outfit that you feel you can fish with confidently, everything else will begin to fall into place.

Presentation is the second most important factor in fly fishing, whether you are on a gin-clear spring creek, a vast fast-flowing Alaskan river or an overgrown brook. This is where the correct combination of rod, line, leader and tippet is so important, enabling you to present your fly in just the right place and in just the right way. In this chapter we will look at the role of each element of your tackle, and the many choices that face you.

THE RIGHT ROD

A good fly rod that suits your purpose and your style of fishing will become your most prized possession and, having said you don't have to spend a fortune, it must be admitted that quality sometimes comes at a price. However, many rods in the $100–$200 range will perform more than satisfactorily.

Below: *Fishing with the rod, reel and line that best suit the size of the water being fished will make presenting your fly to a fish that much easier and more pleasurable.*

Right: *Big rivers require more powerful, but not necessarily longer, 5- or 6-weight rods that will present a fly at a distance, and will also be up to taking control of a fish when hooked at a distance.*

The Keeper Ring

Most fly rods have a small keeper ring, into which to hook your fly when you're not fishing, but in my opinion this is completely unnecessary. I was shown the best way to keep a fly under control when walking along the river bank by a very old instructor many years ago. He hooked his fly into the tip top, or end ring, of his rod, looped the line round his reel and then tightened the line. This takes only moments. When the next fish rose and he wanted to make a cast,

all he had to do was unhook the fly and, because all of his leader and some of the line was outside the tip top, he could start casting without having to pull the rest of his leader and the end of his fly line through the top rings. Whatever you do, don't hook your fly into the cork of the rod handle – this will gradually wreck the cork.

Above: Tree-lined rivers are best fished with short rods because there is likely to be only limited room to cast, and only short casts are required. If you must fish amongst trees but your rod is too long, you can always fish with just the top section (of a two-piece rod) or the top two sections (of a four-piece rod).

The action of a rod – whether it is stiff and has a fast action, or it is softer and has a slower action – is very much a matter of personal choice, and you will only discover which you prefer by using various rods. The stiffness also affects the rod's performance when it comes to playing a fish. A stiff rod may be too unforgiving to protect fine tippets, but a soft one may be unable to cope with the occasional very big fish.

The ideal rod should be able to cast short lines as well as long lines – not every fish will be caught at maximum casting range – and be able to cope with head winds. It's impossible to assess all this when you can only test-cast a rod, so it's helpful if you can find someone who has a similar rod to the one that you're interested in and ask to borrow it. Internet forums can also be a good source of practical fishing information and commentary.

Rod Length

The late Lee Wulff was a great protagonist of short rods and would even fish for – and catch – Atlantic salmon on rods that were only six feet long. A short rod is quick and easy to cast and fish with, and is ideal for making soft and delicate short casts. Short rods can be cast very accurately because the tip is less likely to drift away from the intended backward and forward casting path. For most river fishermen, accuracy and the ability to place a fly precisely at relatively short distances is far more important than being able to cast to the far bank and beyond. Even on very big, wide rivers, short to medium length casts are likely to prove every bit as productive as long shots to that fish rising at the edge of your casting ability. Short rods also have the benefit of being able to apply more pressure on a fish that has been hooked.

Short rods of up to 7 feet, 6 inches are at their best on small streams, where the majority of fish likely to be caught will be small, and on heavily wooded streams and rivers where the river flows through a tunnel beneath the trees, and the only way that you can fish is by getting into the river and wading, flicking a fly to a rising fish or into a likely lie. For any angler who fishes in these conditions on a regular basis, a short rod will be an essential part of his or her armory. However, a short rod's weaknesses are revealed when it comes to casting long distances, lifting a long line off the water or manipulating and mending the line on the water. This is a severe handicap that can render some stretches of water all but unfishable.

A longer rod of between 8 feet and 9 feet will cope much better with a wide range of river sizes, and will also handle adverse weather conditions, such as strong winds, much more capably. If you ever get caught out and find yourself wishing you had that short rod, do what Lefty Kreh used to do and fish with the top half of your rod. Simply take the top section, or the top two sections of a four-piece travel rod, strip off plenty of line from the reel and then tuck the butt and reel into your waders. You can cast and fish very successfully like this when the situation requires it.

Longer rods allow for much better line control on the water and ease of mending your line, as well as making life so much easier when casting over high vegetation and weed growth. Long rods are also excellent for use while nymphing, and when fishing bigger rivers and making longer casts, the extra length will really come into its own.

AFTM Rating

When choosing a rod, length cannot be considered in isolation – one must consider the line weight as well. Every fly rod is rated with an AFTM (American Fishing Tackle Manufacturers) number, which refers to the line weight with which the rod is recommended to be used. Line weight is influenced by the size of fish likely to be caught and the size of flies used.

Lines and rods rated 1 and 2 are only suitable for small nymphs and dry flies, and are unsuitable for fishing big, bushy flies such as Woolly Buggers. From a financial perspective, it's also worth bearing in mind that the choice of very light fly lines is limited, and there are few budget lines available.

A very light-line rod isn't really suitable for catching big fish, particularly on a regular basis, as it may not have the necessary backbone to land the fish, and it is unsporting to try and do so unless you are very confident that you can play a big fish properly on a light rod. It can be done with care and confidence, but you really need to know how to play the fish properly and quickly or the battle will go on so long that you'll exhaust it to death in the water (see Playing and Landing Fish, pages 84-95).

The higher the AFTM rating, the heavier the fly line and the stronger the rod, which means that larger flies can be cast and larger fish can be played. Choose a rod that is appropriate to the kind of fishing you'll be doing. A 5-weight rod is a good happy medium for most forms of trout fishing. While a 2-weight rod can't land a monster salmon, there is no pleasure to be had in playing a 1lb trout on a 10-weight rod!

Below: All fly rods are marked with their length and recommended line weight. Shown here is a Sage XP 8 feet, 6 inches for a 4-weight line.

CHOOSING A REEL

A fly reel can be inexpensive and purely functional, most typically made from plastic or graphite, or it can be a thing of beauty and a pleasure to own and fish with. A quality reel will be machined from bar stock alloy or even space age or aircraft grade material. In principle, all fly reels perform the same basic functions: holding the fly line neatly and allowing line to be stripped-off the spool or arbor smoothly and easily, and rewound as and when necessary, but there's more to it than that.

The most basic type of fly reel has a simple click pawl drag that cannot be adjusted and, unless it works smoothly, this kind of reel is best avoided. When fishing with light lines and fine tippets, you cannot afford to use a reel that might stick, overload and then break your tippet. A simple reel with an exposed rim does at least allow you to add pressure to the rim with your hand to slow a fast-running fish, but a reel with a good, smooth, adjustable drag really comes into play when you are fishing for larger fish, particularly in big rivers with strong currents.

When choosing a reel to suit a 4-weight rod or lighter, I would go for the lightest reel that I could find or afford, and would not worry too much about the drag. For a 5-weight rod, the choice between lightness and a decent drag is not clear cut, but for a 6-weight rod and above, go

Above: For many anglers, a reel is just a means of holding and managing the fly line. But a quality reel with a good adjustable drag system adds to the pleasure and is necessary when fighting large fish.

Below: Although laying a rod in the river alongside a fish makes a good photo, you risk getting grit into the reel as well as soaking the line, backing and rod handle. This is a practice best avoided.

Opposite bottom: Reels can be machined from bar stock aluminium (left) or they can made from graphite (right), along with other synthetic materials.

for a really good drag. My reasoning is based on the fact that a trout up to about three pounds will be played by holding the fly line in your hand, giving and taking line as necessary, so the reel isn't crucial. With a fish above three or four pounds, you will most likely be using the reel to play the fish some of the time, if not all of it, and a good, smooth drag system makes a lot of difference. (If you do buy a reel with an adjustable drag system, turn to page 89 to find out how to set it correctly.)

It makes sense to choose a reel with the largest spool, or arbor (these reels tend to be called 'large arbor' reels in most tackle manufacturers' catalogs). The main benefits of these reels are that they store the line in slightly bigger coils than a reel with a standard arbor, which helps reduce line memory, and the larger diameter provides slightly faster line recovery. From a purely aesthetic perspective, a large arbor reel also looks that much more up to date and earns more bragging rights!

Multiple Lines

Most anglers will probably have more than one fly line, but this does not necessarily require multiple reels. Rather than buying separate reels for each line, it is simpler to just buy additional spools. Not only will this solution save money, but a spool by itself is smaller and lighter to carry in a vest pocket than a complete reel. Then, if you want to change line at any time, you can do so without having to return to your car to fetch a different reel and line.

If you find yourself possessing more fly lines than can be accommodated by your reels and extra spools, it is wise to invest in a line changer. These devices, offered by manufacturers such as Cortland and Tibor, allow anglers to remove the fly line from their reels neatly and efficiently for easy storage. They are relatively inexpensive and quite easy to use.

Above: *Always remove the protective covering from the handle of a new rod before fishing with it. If you don't, it will be harder to hold, and any water that gets between it and the handle may discolor the cork.*

Above: *Small waters and rivers are best fished with light lines, such as a 3- or 4-weight line. Heavier lines will be more difficult to cast the relatively short distances typical of small streams, and will also create more of a disturbance on the water's surface.*

CONSIDERING THE FLY LINE

The choice of fly line is an important consideration. Unfortunately, the range of possibilities appears bewildering, as tackle manufacturers introduce new tapers, different coatings, softer and more supple lines for cold weather, stiffer lines for hotter conditions and longer casts – they are always looking for a gap between line types so that they can fill it with something. However, it is a subject worth researching, as a good line with the right taper will make casting easier, thereby improving presentation and increasing the number of hook-ups.

Fly Line Taper

Fly anglers argue endlessly over whether a double taper (DT) line will cast and present a fly more accurately and delicately than a weight forward (WF) line. Originally, DT lines had finer tip sections than WF lines, but there has been so much design and development work done on WF lines that many of them are now designed for good presentation. A modern WF line can have a very similar forward taper to a DT and will, therefore, cast and deliver the fly in just the same way. This whole discussion may seem a mite esoteric to the average angler, but it is of interest to the more experienced angler with a more expert cast. For the average angler, who can cast competently but not to 'professional' standards, the best line to use is the one that you can cast consistently well. A mediocre cast with your preferred line is always going to be better than a bad cast with one designed for a supposedly superior presentation.

The suppleness of the fly line is another factor to take into account. A supple line will be better for shorter casts and slack-line dry fly casts, while the stiffer lines are usually designed and manufactured for longer casts.

Floating and Sinking

Will you need more than a floating line? For most river and stream fishing, the answer is no: a floater will cover virtually every situation. A floating line is meant to float, and some makes and lines do float much better, and for longer, than others, so choose the best or highest-floating line that you can afford. There is nothing more frustrating than a line that will not float, or a tip that starts sinking just when you don't want it to.

For those occasions when you do want to fish well

below the surface, such as when nymphing or using a streamer, you can use a sinking leader to create a mini sink-tip. These leaders are available in a range of different sink rates, allowing you to choose one that will give the speed of sink to match the water flow, and will get your fly down to the required depth. Anglers who fish well below the surface regularly and in deep water may want to add a sink tip line to their armory: such a line is easier to cast and fish with than a full sinking line. It will be easier to roll cast to bring your fly, or flies, to the surface, and can also be mended, which you cannot do with a sunk line.

Above: Fly lines are available in many different colors, and the choice of which color to use is often personal. However, most fly lines come in bright orange and shades of green.

Color Choices

The last aspect of a fly line to consider is the color, and the choice is largely personal, although in New Zealand the local anglers are obsessed – with good reason – about the importance of line color when stalking big, spooky fish in crystal-clear waters. Certain colors do offer benefits, such as ease of visibility in different light conditions. White and very pale lines will show up well, but they also show the dirt very quickly, and it is not until you have fished with a white line that you appreciate just how dirty a fly line can get. (Perhaps we should all remember to clean our lines regularly, even if they do not look as though they need it. Dirt on a line does affect its casting and fishing performance, reducing its ability to shoot well, and its floatability.)

All in all, a relatively dark or neutral color is to be preferred. Line manufacturers have recognized that some colors are easier to see than others, and they now make lines with different colored tips – often described as a nymph or indicator tip – or they make the head of a weight forward line in one color and the running line another.

Check Your Line

Remember to inspect the end of your fly line regularly, as the hinging that occurs at the end of the joint between line and leader can crack the line coating, allowing water into the core and also weakening it seriously enough to break if you catch a big or hard-fighting fish. As soon as you notice any cracking, simply cut away the damaged part of the line and attach a new leader to the end of your line using your preferred method.

At the end of a day on the river it is advisable to strip off all the line that you have used and rewind it evenly and smoothly, making sure that there are no kinks that might jam and result in a broken tippet the next day. If you don't, or you forget to do this at the end of a day's fishing, make sure that you check everything before you start fishing again, whether it's the next day or a week later. Such simple checks can make the difference between a great day on the water and a day best forgotten.

LEADERS AND TIPPETS

At the business end of the line, the leader acts as a more or less invisible extension of the fly line and a means of attaching a fly to your line. Described as 'a device for deception as well as presentation', the leader plays a vital role in good presentation by smoothly transmitting the energy in the fly line, created by casting, from the line to your fly. A well-designed and constructed leader will also allow your fly to float in a realistic and life-like manner, as though it is not attached to anything. The choice of leader and tippet can be crucial to success, particularly on windy days and, by contrast, when fishing flat, slow streams, the extremes of difficult fishing conditions.

Leader Construction

A leader consists of two main parts: the leader body, which is the long, tapered length fixed to the end of the fly line, and the fine, level tippet between the end of the leader body and the fly. The leader body, made up of the butt and the taper, may be a single length, as in a braided, furled or tapered knotless monofilament leader, or it may be a number of sections of different diameters of monofilament knotted together. The tippet is a replaceable

Below: Pull off a length of tippet material of the appropriate weight for the fly being used and the fish likely to be caught.

Bottom: Always trim the tag end of a knot closely, otherwise it may catch bits of flotsam on the surface of the river.

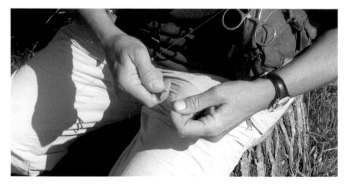

length of nylon, or monofilament, and its strength and diameter should be matched to the size of the fly and the likely size of fish to be caught.

Thinner leaders and tippets cut through the water more quickly than thicker ones, and are also marginally less buoyant, so they will sink more quickly. This may seem a bit academic, but if you are using small nymphs that you want to sink quickly without having to add split shot to the leader, a fine leader may make a significant and essential difference.

KNOTTED LEADERS

The basic tapered leader is a knotted one, and when bought ready-made, these are quick and easy to use. Alternatively you can tie your own, giving you the option of producing leaders matched to specific conditions, incorporating your own, or recognized, proven tapers. Knotted leaders hark back to the days of the drawn gut leader, when gut was only available in short lengths, necessitating knotting together several lengths to produce a leader of sufficient length. The big disadvantage of ready-made or home-tied knotted leaders is, obviously, that they have knots in them. Knots can fail; they reduce a leader's strength, however well they are tied; they increase the visibility of a leader and they catch scum and bits of flotsam on the water surface. Knots break when they slip, so when tying up a leader always lubricate the knots before tightening them carefully, slowly and fully.

KNOTLESS LEADERS

Knotless tapered leaders have the advantage of being completely smooth, and as a result, do not disturb the water much when landing. These leaders are likely to be made from 'double strength' mono, with high strength and small diameter. Although long leaders can be cut at either or both ends to produce a leader with more butt or front-end taper, it is still something of a compromise given the relative inaccuracy of the manufacturing process.

BRAIDED LEADERS

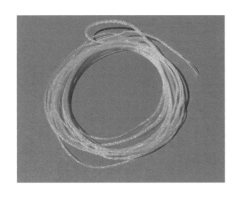

Braided leaders have the big advantage of having no memory, and they are also long lasting. On the down side, they are more visible than mono (although this can be helpful in certain circumstances), and they have a rougher surface than mono and absorb water, which can shower down on the stream surface as you false cast and can spook sensitive fish. They are available in floating or sinking versions, including different sink rates, so you can use one as a mini sink-tip. Braided leaders can be fixed directly to the fly line in the same way as a braided loop.

FURLED LEADERS

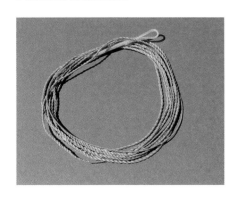

Furled leaders look similar to braided leaders and, to a lesser degree, suffer from the same disadvantage of absorbing water unless kept well greased, but they are a delight to use. A furled leader is the only kind you can cast by hand and get to turn over. This can be the answer to fishing small flies effectively, and also fishing for selective trout, particularly in clear and/or slow water, where a soft, supple leader will give delicacy of presentation. A range of designs is available, and can be made from monofilament, fly tying thread or Kevlar thread as required; each will exhibit slightly different characteristics. A furled leader is made from a single, continuous length of thread that is wrapped in a precise pattern around a series of posts, with more turns round the posts or pylons at the butt end (which produces the required thickness and taper) before all the threads are twisted together for a set number of turns. This can be done by hand or, preferably, with a small electric motor, as a very high number of turns is required. To make two or more leaders the same, the same number of turns

needs to be used. Furled leaders can have a smooth, continuous taper from butt to tip, the taper gradient can be steep or shallow and they can be made with a weight-forward taper if required. They can also be made in colors to match a background, and in two colors, with a section made from a highly visible thread to act as an indicator.

Their natural elasticity protects light tippets, they have good knot strength and are less prone to wind knots, but knots are more difficult to remove. A furled leader can become mildewy unless dried properly.

POLY LEADERS

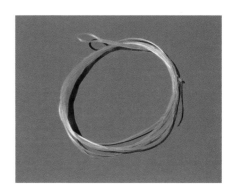

Polyurethane, or 'poly' leaders have a smooth, tapered polyurethane coating over a monofilament core. This is the same material as the fly line, so the leader can match the line's flexibility, giving a smooth transmission of energy through to the fly. The polymer coating comes in different colors, and can be made to produce floating leaders or leaders with different sink rates. A loop in the end of the mono core to which the tippet is attached is usually made.

Fly Line to Leader

The line to leader joint can have a positive or negative effect on the degree of hinging between the end of fly line and start of leader. Whether you nail knot a heavy length of mono to the end of your line, whip a loop on the end or use a braided loop (these are easy to fit, but they do have the disadvantage of possibly holding water), I believe that it is important to make sure that you seal the end of your line with waterproof super-glue. This is to stop water finding its way into the end, because as it works its way up the line it will, sooner or later, make the end of your line sink.

If you have a floating line that sinks, or is reluctant to float for any reason, it may be worth cutting a short length off the tip end and sealing it well. This has worked for me in the past, but if it has no effect, then you should return the line to the manufacturer and ask for a replacement. A floating line should – no, must – float.

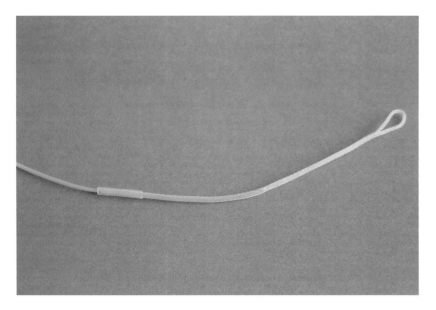

Replacing the Loop

Although a number of fly line manufacturers produce lines with a welded loop on the front end, it is likely that you will need to replace the loop at some time in the future. A new method of making smooth loops in the ends of fly lines, involving the use of heat-shrink tubing, has been developed by a Dutchman, Sepp Fuchs. It is a quick and easy way to make a loop that will slide easily through the rod guides. The same technique can also be used to make loops on the ends of poly leaders. The end of the line is cut at an angle and a loop made, which is threaded through a piece of heat-shrink tubing that is about 2 inches long. The shrink tube is then warmed with a cigarette lighter just enough to make it shrink, but not so much that you melt the coating on the fly line completely. Be warned that it is very easy to over-heat a thin line, such as a 4-weight. As you warm the shrink tube, it shrinks but it also protects the fly line as the two sides of the loop are softened and welded together. You can control the size of the finished loop by applying the heat closer to, or further away from the end of the loop. When the shrink tubing has cooled, cut the open end and peel the tube off the line. You should be left with a very smooth, welded loop that will slide nicely through the rod guides: indeed, a better loop than some manufacturers' early efforts. A similar loop can be made on the reel-end of the line to which the backing is attached.

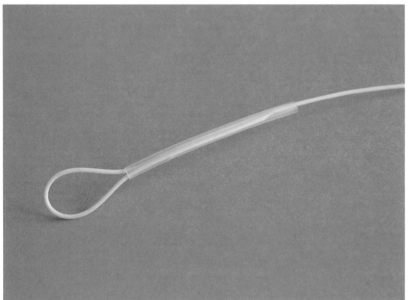

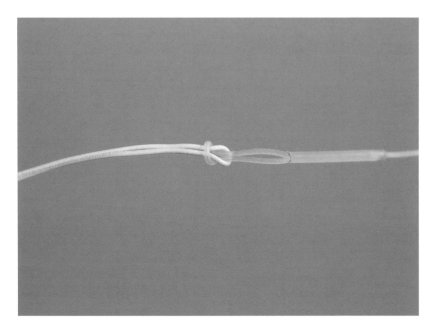

Top: A braided loop, fitted to an orange fly line, is a quick and easy way to attach your line to the leader.

Middle: A neat loop can be made on the end of a fly line using heat-shrink tubing. Heat is applied to the tube, which is removed once the loop is welded together.

Bottom: The loop-to-loop connection is a quick, easy and efficient way to join a leader to a fly line. It is just as easy to remove the leader, should you need to change to a different type.

Leader Design

The wide range of leader types and constructions is both a help and a hindrance. Each type of leader will have its good points and bad points. There is such a multiplicity of leaders available because each manufacturer thinks that its leaders are the best for different types of fishing. Leaders have changed from being all purpose to being ever more specific, whether designed for fishing a particular type of water or catching a certain quarry.

The design of the taper of a leader is crucial to its performance. A taper that is too short is likely to turn over too quickly, and will make your fly land with a splash. If the taper is too long, the leader may be reluctant to turn over at all. Traditional knotted mono and furled leaders can be designed with a straight, progressive taper or a compound taper that mimics the taper of a weight-forward fly line, as has been mentioned earlier. According to the late Charles Ritz, a well-designed leader should be 60 per cent butt, 20 per cent taper and 20 per cent tippet. This formula has stood the test of time and is as good a place as any to start when designing your own leaders. The thickness of the butt of a leader should be between 60 and 75 per cent of the thickness of the end of the fly line, and, if possible, similar in flexibility. You can get an indication of the comparative stiffness of leader butt and fly line by bending a section of each and feeling the resistance. The thickness and stiffness both help transmit and disperse the casting energy, which results in the smooth presentation of your fly.

Below: From top, sections of poly, braided and furled leaders.

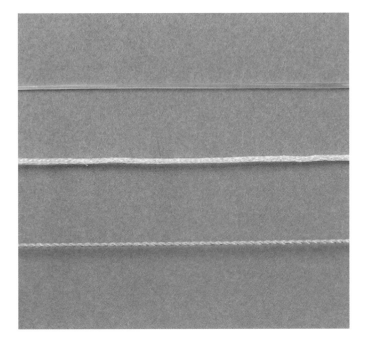

Above: There must be plenty of good trout in this shade, where they await the dropping of terrestrial insects from the branches above. The best fish usually take up the most difficult and challenging lies.

A thicker and stiffer leader will be beneficial when fishing in windy conditions and when using big, bushy flies, as the extra stiffness will help turnover. It will help improve accuracy of presentation in other situations, but may lack a degree of finesse when presenting a small dry fly. Softer leaders are much better for dry fly fishing.

The Importance of Leader Length

It will help your cast if you match the length of your leader to typical casting distances. Long leaders and short casts do not work well because you probably won't have enough line outside the rod tip to load your rod when you cast. Rod action and casting speed will also influence your choice of leader length. You can use a longer leader with a fast rod and fast casts because long, supple leaders need more energy to get them to turn over well. Anglers who cast more slowly, using a slower-action rod, use shorter leaders more successfully. A shorter leader will also help improve your accuracy when casting. A good starting point is to use a leader that is the same length as your rod.

Long leaders can be very effective – and even essential – when fishing in very clear water, particularly on sunny days when the shadow from a fly line will spook

Leader and Tippet Materials

One of the themes running through this book is the importance of using equipment and materials in which you have confidence. Nowhere is this more important than choice of leader and tippet material. Choose a brand that you can knot easily and consistently well, and that matches the manufacturer's strength consistently. Stick to a material or make that you know and trust, even if it is not the very latest material.

fish. The extra-long leader keeps the thick fly line further away from the fish.

Long, fine leaders also have (slightly) more stretch, and thus greater ability to absorb the shock loads of a fish making an unexpected dash for freedom. Very soft leaders and flexible tippets are fine for spring creeks

Below: A wavy leader will give a dry fly a longer drag-free float compared to a straight cast and straight leader.

and similar pellucid flows when presenting a dry fly in calm conditions, but when pin-point accuracy is essential (for example, when nymph fishing), a stiffer leader, particularly the butt section, will turn over better and deliver the fly with greater accuracy. A stiffer leader with a heavier butt section will also make casting into a strong wind easier, as the better turn-over will cut through the wind more easily. Another time when good turn-over and reliable accuracy is of great benefit is

when the light is fading and it starts becoming difficult to see exactly where your fly has landed on the water, particularly if you are fishing very small flies.

It is a good idea to experiment with different leader set-ups until you find one that suits your way of casting and fishing, and the waters that you fish most regularly. Even then you must be prepared to make changes to your set-up in order to suit different or changing conditions. Ready-made knotless tapered leaders can be modified by cutting back either the butt or tippet end, or both ends. If you cut a length off one end only, you will upset the Ritz 60:20:20 formula (see page 23), but it may give the right result. Cutting the tip back will increase the proportion of butt, and so will produce a stiffer leader, whereas cutting the butt end will result in a shorter butt section and a greater proportion of thinner leader. Always keep the pieces of leader that you have cut off so that you can use them to cut another leader to match the one that you have just trimmed to length.

Tying Your Own

If you decide to tie your own leaders, don't try to knot together two pieces of material that are more than 0.002 or 0.003 inches different in diameter, as they cannot be knotted together successfully and may also cause the leader to hinge, hampering good energy transfer and

Above: *When really delicate presentation is crucial – particularly when fishing a dry fly – consider using either a furled leader or a leader built to one of George Harvey's slack-line leader specifications.*

turnover. Recognized leader formulae will take this into account. The forward end can be finished with a loop to which you attach the tippet using the loop-to-loop connection (see page 22). If you don't have such a loop, the leader will get shorter and thicker each time you cut the end of the leader to change the tippet, and over time this will have an adverse effect on casting and presentation. An alternative to a loop is to add a short sacrificial length of mono to which the tippet is tied. When this length is too short to knot, simply cut it off and replace it.

Dry-fly fishermen who are after perfect casts that present the fly with the minimum of disturbance should consider using furled leaders or hand-tied leaders to a formula such as the well known George Harvey's slack-line leader, which presents a fly in a wonderful series of S-curves.

Nylon Monofilament

Standard nylon monofilament has been around a long time now. It knots well and is usually up to the indicated strength. It has a specific gravity of 1.15, compared to that of water of 1.00, so when greased it will float and if degreased it will sink. Handling monofilament with greasy fingers can be enough to stop it sinking when required. Nylon has a better strength-to-diameter ratio than fluorocarbon (see below), but is damaged by exposure to sunlight and absorbs water after long submersion. It has good abrasion resistance and knot strength, but it loses some of its stretch if exposed to heat or ultra-violet light. As nylon can be affected by poor storage in a tackle shop, always check on the age of a spool, if at all possible, before buying.

Double-strength monofilament has its advocates as well as its detractors. It can be difficult to knot initially, but it does offer a thinner leader or tippet for a given breaking strain, or a stronger tippet at no increase in material diameter.

Copolymer is nylon reinforced with resin to produce a stronger, thinner material. It can be made with a low specific gravity so that it will float well, which makes it good for dry fly fishing. It can also be double-stretched to make it double strength.

Fluorocarbon

Fluorocarbon is made from polyvinylidene fluoride (PVDF), which was invented in 1978. It is less visible in water and sinks more quickly than nylon due to its high specific gravity of 1.72. This makes it an ideal tippet material for nymph fishing, but it should be used with due caution for dry-fly fishing as it may pull your fly underwater. It has a refractive index that makes it almost invisible to fish, and some manufacturers claim that it is more resistant to UV light and more abrasion-resistant than nylon. It is also inert, which makes it resistant to chemicals.

Fluorocarbon is inherently much stiffer than nylon, and to reduce the stiffness, some knot and tensile strength has to be sacrificed. Fluorocarbon does not absorb water, so its wet and dry knot strengths are more or less the same.

Below: *It is important to use the correct size of tippet to match the size of fly being fished, particularly when using big, bushy flies, although it is less important with smaller flies.*

The Tippet

The thickness or diameter of the tippet is determined by the size of fly to be fished. A thin tippet will not turn over properly when fished with a large bushy fly, and too thick a tippet will not allow a small fly to float or swim reasonably naturally. Equally, the softness, or flexibility, of the tippet can affect the movement and mobility of a nymph.

MATCHING TIPPET AND FLY

Your tippet needs to be strong enough to hold and land a big fish, particularly in heavy water, and it should be matched to the size of fly that you are fishing. Rarely will it be true that if a tippet is strong enough to land a fish, it will be too thick to fool it. While there will always be circumstances that demand a very fine tippet, fishing too fine a tippet may mean that you cannot bring a big fish to hand to release without the risk of killing it through exhaustion. Using a heavier tippet will reduce break-offs, and if it proves to be too thick then you can always use a thinner tippet. If you lose a fish through a break-off, check the end of the tippet. If it is curly like a pig's tail, then the knot failed. If, however, the end is straight and clean, this indicates that the tippet failed and broke.

THE NUMBERS RULES

To help get a good match of tippet strength to fly size, you need to know the Rule of Four. The correct choice will mean that you have a tippet with the power to turn over properly, and yet still be soft enough to allow the fly to float or drift as naturally as possible. If you want to fish a size 12 fly, what is the optimum tippet size? Divide 12 by four and you get three, or 3X, and that is the designation of the correct tippet. Working the rule the other way, if you have a 4X tippet, the Rule of Four says that when you multiply four by four you get 16, and that is the correct hook size to use with your 4X tippet. Where this rule falls down is when using large bushy flies, such as Grey Wulffs, which need a heavier tippet to balance them.

The Delicate Approach

If you don't want to use an extra-long leader when fishing for spooky fish, try using a longer tippet. It is quicker and easier to add a long tippet than it is to change to a different leader, and an overly long tippet can be cut back when it is no longer needed.

If you know the diameter of your line, rather than the X-factor, the Rule of Eleven will convert the diameter of your tippet material, in thousands of an inch, to an X figure. For example, a tippet material of .006 inches should be treated as a whole number, six, which is then subtracted from 11, giving you 5, or 5X.

Below: The tippet needs to be strong enough to bring a fish to hand so that it can be released, but it also needs to match the size of the fly that you are using.

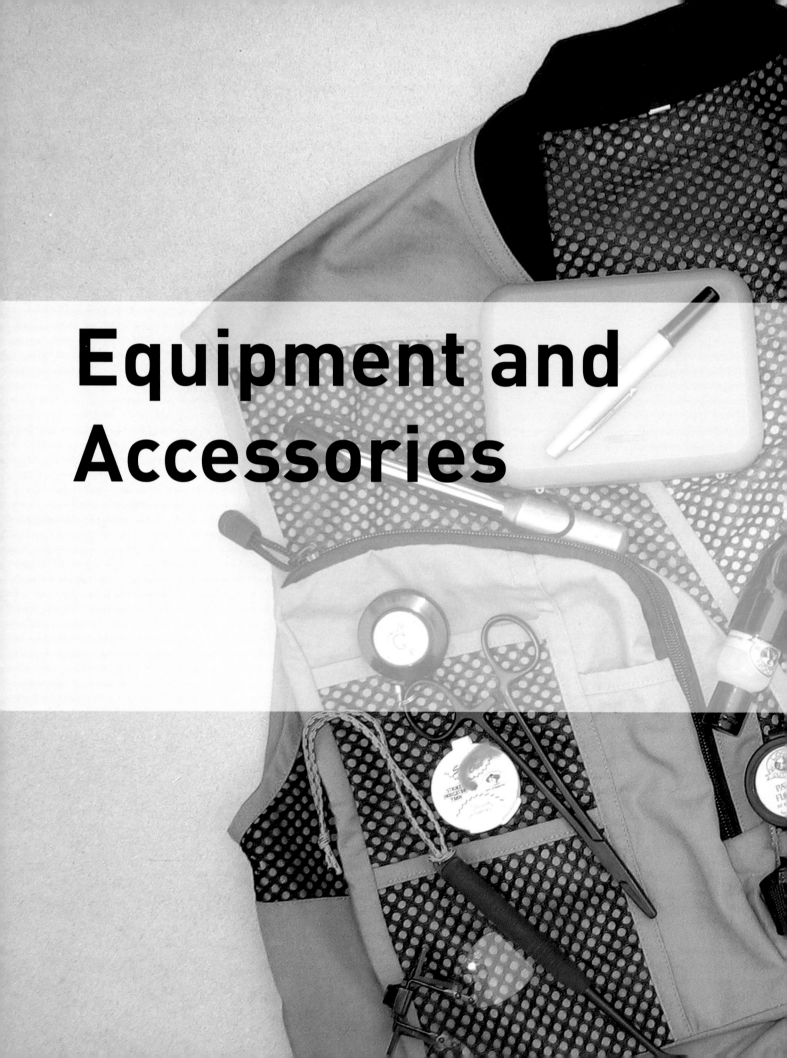

Equipment and Accessories

Equipment and Accessories

It's all too easy to buy more accessories than you need, and there are many items that are of little practical use. However, when chosen with care, good accessories are nice to own as well as use. One of the keys to successful fly fishing is being organized when you're on the river – having the right line, the right equipment and the right fly with you, and being able to find and use them all quickly. What could be more frustrating than trying to change a fly in a hurry when you can't find the right pattern, or fumbling through endless pockets searching for a new tippet? In this chapter we look at the essential equipment and accessories, and also at how to arrange things so that you can lay your hands on the item you need the moment you need it.

BITS AND PIECES

A quick flick through almost any fishing tackle catalog will show an angler far more small accessories than most will know what to do with, let alone have the strength to carry to the river bank or the money to pay for. Many accessories for sale are, in truth, a waste of time, money and space, but a number of small items are essential.

Clippers

A leader clipper, preferably with either a fixed or slide-out needle to clear hook eyes, is essential so that leaders and tippets can be cut or trimmed quickly and neatly. Attach it to the front of your fishing vest with a

Below: A good leader clipper will make quick work of cutting a length of tippet material or the tag-end of a knot.

pin-on reel or zinger. It will always be to hand and you won't lose it.

Unhooking Tools

A pair of forceps (also known as surgical clamps or a hemostat) or a special release tool such as a Ketchum Release is important when you want to be able to unhook a fish quickly and with the minimum of damage. Forceps have the advantage that you can take hold of the hook by the bend and either twist it out of the fish or let the fish kick itself free. This technique seems to work much better with small trout than larger fish, which often require more manipulation to free them. The Ketchum Release has many advocates, but to use one successfully does rely on holding the leader tight with your rod, or taking hold of the tippet with one hand, while you slide the tool down the tippet and over the fly in the fish's mouth or jaw before pushing the hook free. Holding a fine tippet does run the risk of a break if the fish starts struggling, but, after some practice, using one successfully should not be a problem.

Below: Matte black is a good color for forceps (left), as they will not flash in the sun. A Ketchum Release, designed specially for unhooking fish (right).

Above: Using a pair of forceps to unhook a nice brown trout.

Below: Interlocking spools make a very efficient tippet dispenser.

Storing Tippets

Spare tippet material, in a variety of thicknesses or breaking strains, can be carried either in a special tippet dispenser or on a series of spools that snap together or interlock, which is the cheapest and most efficient method. If your favorite material is sold on spools that don't lock together, it is worth buying as many spools as you need of a brand that has locking spools and either using that brand and then replacing the material with your preferred brand, or scrapping it in the first place

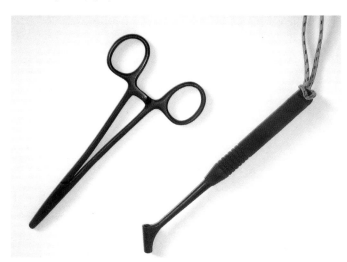

and replacing it with your preferred choice. Tie loops on the ends of the tippet material before you leave home, as that will be one less thing to do on the river.

Floatant

There is a wide range of fly and leader floatants available. Paste-type fly floatants are good in warm weather and when your fingers are warm enough to turn the paste into liquid, but in cold weather consider using a liquid. Fly floatants, which are likely to be used regularly, are best carried in 'bottom up' carriers, or caddies, clipped to your vest. Line floatant can be carried in an outside vest pocket.

Last Rites

If you do intend to kill a fish, you must dispatch it quickly and cleanly, and a "priest" (a short stout wooden rod) is the best instrument to use. Don't try to kill a fish by hitting it with the landing net handle, a stone or whatever comes to hand. Treat it with the respect it deserves and administer the last rites with the proper tool. Even if you do not want to kill a fish, you may catch one that is badly injured or you might injure a fish when trying to

unhook it. To return a fish that is bleeding badly is to consign it to a lingering death, so don't let this happen: put it out of its misery.

Strike Indicators

Strike or bite indicators are useful for the nymph fisher who has difficulty detecting takes. Strike indicators can be either the putty type, where a pinch of fluorescent colored putty is squeezed and rolled onto the leader, or bright fluorescent synthetic yarn, treated to make it float, that can be tied onto the leader in the appropriate position. Putty works well on flat waters, whereas a piece of yarn is better on rougher water, as it will float much higher. Yarn tends to be more visible in strong sunlight.

Not Essential, But...

You can certainly manage without them, but there are a few items that I always carry with me on fishing trips, and these have proven their usefulness time after time. A small seine net that can be dragged through the water will help you to find out what nymphs and adults are in the river, and enable you to determine which fly you should be using. A thermometer will give you invaluable infor-

Below: A seine net is an invaluable way of finding out what type of food there is in a river. This example is stored in a little bag on a landing net, ready for use (see page 71).

Below: A thermometer can help you find cooler waters or a spring on a day when water temperatures are high. Some also incorporate a holder for waste leader material and a magnet for retrieving lost flies.

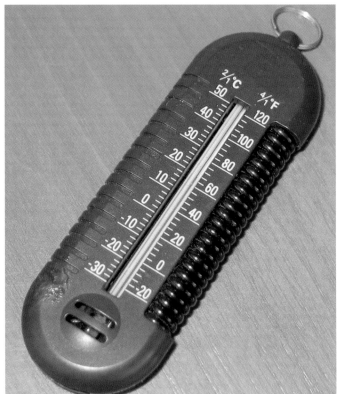

mation about the water, and the more you use it the more you'll be able to correlate the temperature with what is happening in the river. Some clever thermometers even incorporate a waste leader material holder and a magnet for retrieving lost flies or extracting one from a fly box. Another handy accessory is a small flashlight, which will help when you're tying on flies at twilight. It can also help to guide you home when you've carried on casting just that bit too long!

Keeping a Note

A final thought on small accessories is to suggest carrying a note pad and pen, if not in your vest then in your car. This way, either during or at the end of the day you can make notes about interesting or significant things that you saw or happened, any tackle repairs needed or flies that need to be bought or tied to replenish your fly boxes.

POLARIZED SUNGLASSES

No angler, especially a fly angler, should be without polarized sunglasses. By cutting out reflected light, they allow you to see through the surface of the water to what is happening below and, almost equally importantly, they provide protection for your eyes from an errant fly when casting, particularly in strong winds.

Good fishing glasses should fit well, be comfortable to wear and designed to prevent light entering from the sides. This can be achieved by flat glasses with separate

Above: Polarized sunglasses allow the angler to see into the water, and also provide protection from an errant fly when casting, particularly in strong winds. Tan or brown lenses increase contrast and are good all-round fishing colors.

side pieces or a curved wrap-around design, but be aware that wrap-around glasses that fit tightly to your face may be so heavily curved that they distort and magnify your view.

Lens Quality

To tell whether lenses are polarized or not, hold them in front of you and look at something shiny. If, as you turn the lenses, the shine disappears or is reduced, then the lenses are polarized. If nothing happens, they are not. You can perform a similar test to check the optical quality of the lenses. Hold the glasses at arm's length and look through them, with one eye closed, at a vertical line. Now move the glasses from side to side. If the vertical line bends or wiggles, then the optical quality of the lenses is not ideal and could cause eye strain.

Lenses can be either glass or polycarbonate. Glass provides the highest optical quality, better polarization, photochromic capability and the best scratch resistance. Polarized glass lenses are hand made, and the polarizing filter is thicker than that used with plastic lenses. The result is better quality glasses and a higher price.

Glasses with polycarbonate or plastic lenses are

light, durable and cheaper to make. Some are said to be scratch resistant, but they will scratch if abused (as will glass if mistreated badly). Good glasses deserve to be kept in a good case when they are not being worn.

Lenses should provide 100 per cent ultraviolet (UV) protection. If in doubt, do check before buying. Good glasses should also protect against infra red, and top-quality polarized lenses will cut out up to 99 per cent of reflected light. Lightweight glasses will be more comfortable to wear for a long time, and thin frames will have fewer blind spots.

Lens Color

Fish often reflect their surroundings, which can make them difficult to see in the water. A fish's shadow on the river bed may be the one thing that gives away its presence, and the correct choice of lens color can enhance shadows in water as well as reducing reflected light from the river surface. Blue lenses reduce shadows so they will make it harder to spot fish, but a color that neutralizes blue light will help enhance contrast. For this

Below: When looking for fish in a river, you need to look through the water into the river, not just at it. Trout have the ability to blend in with their surroundings, often making them difficult to see. This is when polarized sunglasses are needed.

reason, copper, vermilion or amber tints, which provide high contrast, are excellent for sight fishing or stalking. Yellow lenses are only of any use on very dull days, or in low light conditions as darkness falls. Grey lenses are good for bright, sunny days and, as they transmit all colors evenly, there is no color distortion. Tan or brown lenses increase contrast and are good all-round fishing colors.

Other Visual Aids

It is far easier to spot fish in the water when wearing a hat, together with glasses that have wide side-pieces. The aim is to stop unwanted light from coming in from the side, above or behind you, and getting into you eyes. If your glasses don't have side pieces though, and you find that light gets round the side of your glasses, try shielding the side of your face using your hands.

Anglers with failing eyesight who need glasses for close work such as changing flies might consider a pair of fishing glasses with a built-in clear magnifying lens. This will save fumbling in a pocket for reading or magnifying glasses which can then be dropped, or put down and left behind. Another approach is to purchase a pair of magnifier clip-on lenses that can be flipped up out of the way when fishing, or attached to the peak of a cap and raised and lowered as required.

LANDING NETS

Although some anglers never use one, it can be easier to use a net to hold a fish in the water while you unhook it, keeping it at least half in the water. Landing nets come in all shapes, sizes, styles and materials, but any net should have a soft, knotless bag that will do the least harm to any fish that you do net. There are so-called catch and release nets that have either very soft net, or one made of stretchy rubber. The fine mesh used for these nets eliminates the possibility of a fish getting caught up in the holes.

Net Design

Rigid, fixed-frame landing nets are better than the folding kind, which are too prone to collapsing at the wrong moment – assuming they opened properly in the first place. A rigid frame can also be used for extracting fish from weeds. Short-handled, wooden tennis racket-style nets are very popular for wading or when fishing rivers with very low banks. They have the great virtue of simplicity, but you are limited in how far you can reach to net a fish. A more universal, all-round net needs a longer handle so that you can net a fish from the bank. Extending handles are not always as clever as they may seem, and can become jammed at the wrong moment.

Choose a net where the bag is not too deep, as this will reduce the chances of your fly getting caught in the mesh before you can remove it from a fish. The bag needs only to be deep enough to hold a fish without it being able to jump out.

Above: Landing nets should have soft, knot-free mesh to reduce the chances of damaging a fish's skin.

Below: A tennis racket-style net clipped to this angler's vest with a two-part magnetic holder. These nets are ideal for use when wading.

Multipurpose Nets

Some nets accomplish more than one task simultaneously, and these are obviously very useful. You may want to consider the option of a net that actually weighs the fish, one that has a measuring scale printed on the inside of the net, or one with an 'insect screen' bottom that can be used to catch nymphs and bugs for closer inspection.

A weighing or measuring net – which works by adding together the numbers at the head and tail of the fish to give you its overall length – is ideal for the angler who wants a reasonably reliable indication of the size of the fish caught. Both types of net allow this to be done with the fish in the net, and without causing the fish undue stress.

Fitting a Quick-Seine net to a tennis racket-style net will allow you to use the net as a seine net, letting you sample the bugs and insects in the river. An alternative is to buy a net with a special white, fine mesh section at the bottom, against which nymphs, shrimps and larvae can be easily seen for identification purposes.

Having it Ready

Once you have decided on the type and size of net that you require, the next thing to consider is how to carry it so that it is always ready for action, and so it cannot be

A Helping Hand?

If someone offers to net a fish for you and you accept, you run the risk of the helper rushing to get the fish in the net. This may spur the fish into making one last burst for freedom, or the happy netter may break the tippet or even dislodge your fly from the fish's mouth. If you do allow a fellow angler to help, simply ask him or her to place the net in the water, keep it still while you draw the fish over it and then raise it, hopefully with the fish well inside.

lost. These considerations are especially important when wading. Attaching your net to a D-ring on the back of your vest or chest pack will keep it out of the way, yet still accessible. A magnetic net holder, with a lanyard, will allow your net to be detached by a simple pull, and

Below: After being gently unhooked, this fish is now ready to be returned safely to its natural environment.

the lanyard will keep it attached so that you can't put it down and then walk off without it. A retractor or heavy-duty pin-on reel with a long cord is another good alternative, and it has the added benefit that when you let go of your net, the cord will retract it. Another option, the dog-lead type of clip, is strong and reliable, but it requires you to unclip and re-clip the net with one hand, which can be awkward.

CARRYING EVERYTHING

Traditional tackle bags and wicker creels have an old-fashioned charm, but as far as practicality is concerned, they are best consigned to a decorative role. They have too few pockets to allow any proper organization of tackle and accessories, and the single shoulder strap places all the weight on one shoulder, which is both inefficient and uncomfortable.

Modern materials and design have opened up new possibilities, and a fishing vest or chest pack has got to be the right choice. (The chest pack is the more advanced option, but they make my shoulders ache; I just use an old mesh vest.) The angler who anticipates doing any serious, deep wading should buy a short vest, often sold as a wading vest.

Mesh vests have a lot to recommend them, as they are that much cooler in hot weather and it is easy to add an extra layer underneath them on a cool day to keep warm. Strap fastenings are also cooler than a zip, and possibly more durable.

Fishing vests are all about pockets, and I would recommend buying one that has a big pocket on the back that can be used to carry food, drink or a lightweight wading jacket or rain shell if rain is likely. Paradoxically, most vests have too many pockets, guaranteeing that you will lose things, so don't get too carried away with a desire for more pockets.

The Organized Vest

How you load your vest or chest pack will depend on whether you are right- or left-handed, as you want the things that are used most to be easily accessible with your non-rod hand. Once you have worked out how best to stow everything, always return items to the pocket from which they came. No doubt your preferred layout will evolve, but this way you can always find what you are looking for in a hurry or when you are under pressure.

Below: Backpack-style vests are better than traditional vests or tackle bags for carrying lots of gear. In fact, larger vests and chest packs have enough space to accommodate everything you need to prepare yourself for a long day of fishing: a camera, water, food, and a rain shell.

Organizing Your Flies

If you want to spend more time with your fly on the water and less time rummaging around in vest pockets and fly boxes, then organizing your flies is a crucial key. What could be worse than wanting to change the fly quickly, perhaps in fading light, with fish rising all around, and being unable to find the right pattern? Many anglers probably carry far more flies than they need, and the more you carry, the more important it is to organize them properly. And while you are organizing them, you may find that you don't need to carry so many boxes after all. Four or five should be enough for most anglers.

PREPARING FOR THE TRIP

If you are the sort of person who grabs his or her gear at the last minute and rushes off to the river, only to arrive on the bank minus some crucial item, you should make yourself a check list and then make sure that you check everything against it as you load your car or truck. You could even stick the list somewhere visible in your car

trunk. When loading the back of my car I always put my waders, wading boots and landing net (which all live in the garage) on one side; on the other side, my vest, rod, reel and sunglasses all go in together, then food and drink, if needed, followed by spare clothing or a wading jacket if rain is likely, and any other odds and ends. This way I am pretty confident that I will arrive at the river with everything that I will need, although I confess I have had the odd system failure!

From One Extreme...

A good friend who, in my opinion, is singularly badly organized, once produced half a dozen little cardboard boxes from his old-fashioned fishing bag. The boxes were the ones in which the shop that sold him the flies had put them. He hadn't even got round to putting them in his fly boxes, which I do know he possesses. If he had dropped one of the boxes in the water, would he have caught it before it floated away or sank? Returned to his bag, dripping wet, it would no doubt have ended up a soggy mess.

Left: Once you have organized all your flies and boxes, it is important to return each of the flies to their proper places after you have used them. Always replace any flies that you have lost, or that are too badly damaged to be used again.

...To the Other

One of the most complex systems of fly management that I have ever read about involved the originator of the system having a number of mayfly boxes according to species and then according to each stage of emergence; then boxes with seasonal groupings for two or more hatch matching systems; then single boxes for each stage of emergence for the most important and prolific fly hatches on this man's local river.

His midge boxes included cluster midges, adult and transitional midges, all arranged according to color and stage; then there was a terrestrial box, a box of generic 'go to' nymphs, a caddis box containing some 200 flies representing the larvae, pupae, active adults and spent adults of six or seven species, and a box of streamers. He carries anything up to 18 boxes in his fishing vest, with more in reserve in his truck.

Is this fishing for fun? My admiration for someone who can go to such lengths and complexity is tempered by a degree of concern for his sanity!

A Matter of Preference

Which system to choose to organize flies and boxes is down to the individual angler and his or her mentality. Some people are born organizers and others have to work at it. Some will be very happy with a simple and basic system – a box for nymphs, another for dry flies and perhaps a third for big, bushy dry flies. Other will have hundreds of flies in many different patterns and dozens of boxes. Every angler should consider having a box of essential 'go to' or 'must have' flies – the flies that one would never want to fish without.

Types of Fly Box

Before you can start organizing your flies into their boxes, you will need to decide what kind of boxes you want to use. If you have a tendency to drop things, consider investing in waterproof, floating boxes as these can be rescued from the river more easily than boxes that sink, and they will keep your flies dry. Boxes, whether plastic or metal, with foam inserts have much to recommend them. Flies are hooked into the foam, which holds them in place and prevents them from being blown out by the wind, separated into orderly rows so that you can see easily what you have in the box. Flat foam is good for nymphs, but small dry flies are best kept in a ripple foam box. Slitted foam is better still, as the flies can be slotted into the micro-slits, which hold them firmly without them actually being hooked into the foam. The constant action of hooking flies into foam and then removing them, often with a tiny bit of foam caught on the barb, makes ever-bigger holes in flat or ripple foam and eventually destroys it.

Below: A partly filled box with space for many more flies. This is an ideal type of box, as it holds each fly firmly and neatly within a slit in the foam pads.

Traditional aluminum fly boxes with spring lids covering each compartment are perhaps best reserved for big, bushy dry flies such as Grey Wulffs and similar large mayfly imitations so that they don't get crushed. Small flies kept in these boxes will tend to end up hooked together in a tangled clump. Be aware that if you drop one of these boxes with a compartment open you risk losing a lot of flies, and a gust of wind may very well scatter the contents.

Threader boxes with fine wire loops that are loaded with flies at home before going to the river may make life easier for those with failing eyesight. To use one of these systems, the end of the tippet is passed through the wire loop with the right fly on it, and the fly is then pulled off the wire and onto the tippet.

Developing a System

A basic system can be organized along the following lines: a dry fly box, a nymph box and one for big, bushy dries and 'must have' flies. The next stage is to divide

nymphs into weighted and unweighted patterns, or weighted and heavily-weighted. After that, consider having a box for terrestrials and another for streamers. Dry flies could be organized into boxes with representatives of the different stages of a particular natural, from emerger to spinner. Finally, the travelling angler might want to add an all-purpose box of flies.

The best way to arrange flies is in rows by types or patterns, and in sizes from largest to smallest. How many of each pattern should you to take on the water with you? I would say at least half a dozen of your favorite patterns and a minimum of three each of others. Many anglers would double both numbers. You need to have replacements for when a fly is lost, a hook breaks, the fly is chewed beyond use or you need to give one to a companion. I know that well-used flies are often the best, but the time does come when they can be chewed beyond use.

As a regular nymph fisherman I have with me a box of my favorite and most used nymphs, and two boxes for dry flies. I now have a separate box for CDC flies, and between May and the end of July I also carry a compartment box for mayfly (*E. danica*) imitations. You might

Below: A heart-stopping moment as a fine fish closes in on an angler's fly. Will it take the fly or turn away at the last second?

want to have a box just for old favorites, the flies in which you have most confidence and that you always turn to when you are having a hard time catching fish. Another box could, perhaps, contain a selection of nymphs, emergers and dry flies, a match-the-hatch box to cover the flies that you are most likely to encounter on your local river or still water.

Organizing your fly boxes can be done during the closed season. It goes without saying that once you have organized all of your flies and boxes, it is important to return used flies to their proper places.

Fly Care

If you drop a box into the water and it is not waterproof, be sure to leave it open and let the flies inside dry. This will help stop the hooks rusting. Equally, try to dry flies before returning them to their proper boxes. Nymphs and sparsely-dressed flies can be squeezed between your fingers, while bushy ones can be blown on or dried with a piece of amadou or a handkerchief. Alternatively, you can leave them on a fly patch to dry and then put them back in their proper boxes at the end of the day or when you are at home.

Above: A fish taking an emerger pattern hanging in the surface film.

Below: Always make a point of drying flies before returning them to their box. Bushy flies can be dried using either a handkerchief or a piece of amadou.

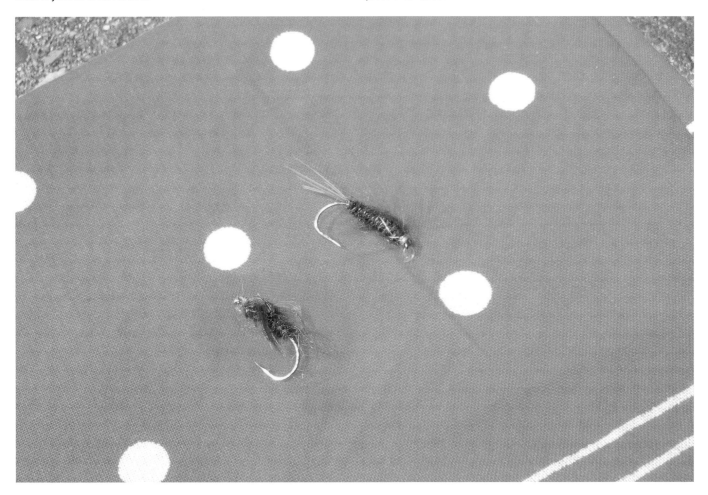

Wading

Wading

Wading is an essential part of fly fishing for trout. In many cases it is impossible to execute a cast from a river bank due to bankside brush and trees. Furthermore, the trout are often located in places that are simply impossible to reach any means other than by getting your feet wet to reach a good casting position. But on streams with steep banks and thick vegetation, wading is the primary means of moving from one stretch of the river to the next. On rivers like this I prefer to enter the river and fish my way upstream rather than heading downstream. This way, I am not fighting the current when I wade back to where I entered the river. Besides the purely practical function that wading serves, there is also a sense of satisfaction – and understanding – to be gained from being in the water with the fish, feeling the current and the riverbed. In this chapter we look at the different kinds of rivers, at the pros and cons of wading and the equipment, the techniques and the all-important safety issues.

WADING EQUIPMENT

To wade successfully and safely you need the right equipment; you also need competent wading skills and confidence. If you have all of these things, then you can wade more adventurously and fish waters ignored by those who are less skilful. As well as a good pair of waders, it is vital to have the right wading boots and soles (or soles on boot-foot waders), a wading stick or staff and a pair of polarized sunglasses. The choice of waders and footwear are particularly vital when wading in powerful, rocky rivers.

Waders

Breathable chest waders are so effective and comfortable to wear that I see little point in using anything else. You can wade deeper than with hip boots, and, when you are not wading, they will keep you dry when it's raining, or when you're walking through wet bankside vegetation. Even in warm weather you won't get

Below: Wading lets you really be at one with the water – a powerful feeling. It also gets you closer to the fish. A hat will cut surface glare and afford better vision through the water's surface.

Above: When selecting a pair of wading boots, make sure that you select the right type of sole, and that the boots are easy to put on and take off.

too over-heated, which cannot be said of neoprene or rubber waders.

Wading Boots

Comfort, grip and support are important qualities in wading boots, especially when wading in deep water or on a rocky river bed. Very light boots may well lack sufficient strength and durability, and may provide only little support and foot protection. Such boots are only good for infrequent use or wading in low-velocity waters.

Medium-weight, hiking boot-style wading boots are very good when you know that you will be covering a lot of ground out of the water, as well as in. Soles with a rubber-tipped heel and toe or sticky rubber will provide a better grip than plain felt soles, which can be slippery on wet grass and sloping river banks. Studded felt or sticky rubber AquaStealth soles will provide good grip in most situations.

Try to select a pair of boots on which the soles do not stick out beyond the width of the foot, as that part of the sole can get stuck between rocks. The soles bend as you push your foot down, but can stick firm when you try to lift your foot again. It is also worth checking that you will be able to undo the laces with cold or frozen fingers. The temperature does not have to be very low for you to end up with numb fingers.

Wading Stick

When wading starts to get serious, a wading stick is essential. In fact, it is asking for trouble not to use one. Although some stick manufacturers describe folding wading sticks as emergency sticks, with careful selection it is possible to buy such a stick for regular use. Some folding sticks are not stiff or strong enough, some have such loose joints that they vibrate uncontrollably in a heavy current, and on some of them the shock-cord is not strong enough to extract the stick when it is jammed between rocks without it coming apart. It goes without saying that you should never buy such a stick!

Below: A wading stick and a means of attaching it to you so that you can let go of it when casting or playing a fish, are essential when doing any serious wading.

Above: A gentle river that should present few wading challenges or hazards apart from an unseen or unsuspected deep hole.

A good folding wading stick will have:
• Joints that are a tight fit and will not pull apart too easily.
• A weighted end that stops the end of the stick floating up as you wade and ensures that when not in use it will hang at your side handle up, making it easier to get hold of when you need to use it.
• A comfortable handle that provides a secure grip.
• A pointed metal end to grip on rocks.

So that you don't loose your stick when you drop it (and you will!) you can attach it to either a wading belt or your vest with a length of shock cord or a heavy-duty pin-on reel or zinger. There are models made for this very purpose. If you use a length of shock cord, keep it fairly short. If it is too long it will allow the handle of the stick to float out of reach.

Staying Afloat

Another item of wading equipment that is being seen more and more, especially on big Western rivers where the wading can be difficult, is the personal flotation device or PFD. If you get upended in a rushing river, it's good to know that at least your head will stay above the water. A PFD can take the form of a simple buoyancy aid, a life jacket or a wading jacket or fishing vest with a built-in life jacket. The difference between a buoyancy aid and a lifejacket is that the latter will turn an unconscious angler onto his or her back and keep the mouth clear of the water so that he or she can breath. A buoyancy aid provides buoyancy only, which may be enough if you are strong, conscious and a good swimmer.

If you are thinking of buying something that is described as a life jacket, it is worth checking that it actually is what it says it is. This is an area in which you get what you pay for. A standard PFD is manually inflated by pulling on a toggle. The more expensive models are fully automatic and inflate within seconds of being submerged. Most are small and unobtrusive enough to be worn with a standard fishing vest. A wading jacket or fishing vest with a built-in device is much more expensive than a simple PFD, but if you intend to wade difficult waters often, it may be worth the investment.

WADING TECHNIQUES

The way in which you wade, and the precautions you need to take, depend very much upon the water you find yourself in. Wading in small streams requires more stealth than in bigger rivers, as there is less water to absorb and dissipate the disturbance that you make, however careful you are. It's not only bad wading to stir-up the river bed and send great ripples across the water in front of you, but thoughtless as well. Wade like this and you will wonder where all the fish have gone. I have both seen and heard waders – fishing friends, no less – who make a noise like an approaching water buffalo. Such a performance is enough to frighten a fellow angler, let alone every fish for miles up and down stream!

Shallow Waters

Wading in shallow, relatively slow flowing rivers and streams should be straightforward and free from drama, unless there is an unexpected hole or hidden fallen branch in the water, which there may well be. Even a fairly smooth river bed, covered in stones, small

pieces of rock and patches of sand and gravel will have the odd large boulder waiting to up-end the unwary angler in too much of a hurry. The minute that you try to move too fast, you risk tripping or stumbling over an unseen hazard, so always wade slowly.

Tougher Conditions

By contrast with small rivers and streams, wading in big, turbulent Western rivers is another matter altogether and needs to be taken very seriously.

I once had an unpleasant experience in a big, powerful river some years ago. John Gierach applied the descriptive phrase 'heart-attack-style wading' to this type of water. Although it was midsummer, the weather was gloomy under a cloudy sky. I had waded quite a long way from where I had got into the river and was out of sight of the two other people fishing with me. The river bed was covered in round boulders and rocks so big that I had to find a way around them. Some were safe to stand on, but sometimes I would get a foot stuck between two or more and would have to retreat to wiggle it free. As I advanced, the river started to get deeper and I decided that it was time to get out, but the closest bank was very inhospitable, with trees and thick brush right to the edge of the water. There were no obvious places to get out. As the river had been used for logging, there were sunken tree trunks to add to the hazards as I made my way along the river. I am pleased to say that I made my way out safely, without a dunking,

Above and Below: *Big, fast-flowing rivers provide what John Gierach described so memorably as 'heart-attack-style wading'. Not only do you have fast water to deal with, but also uneven rock- and boulder-strewn river beds that will trip the unwary. Always use a wading stick, and consider wearing a flotation device if you are at all nervous about falling in. Don't wade out farther than is essential.*

Above: Keep close to the bank when wading as you will be less obvious to the fish in the river.

Below: Where a river has high banks, it may be the case that the only way to fish a stretch of the water is to wade.

and eventually managed to climb out of the river and up the bank. I was very relieved to be back on dry land again. The lessons that I learned that day were to stick within one's limits, not to try to be too adventurous and

if you feel that you are heading into trouble, admit it and get back to the bank before you lose your footing.

Under Pressure

When wading and fishing in heavy water and strong currents, try to keep sideways to the flow, as this reduces the area of your legs or body exposed to the full current and gives you a little less resistance. When facing squarely up- or downstream you are exposed to the full strength of the current. Before you move a foot, use your wading stick to feel your way and find the next foothold. Only move when you are confident about where you are going to put your foot. Try not to put your full weight on the foot that you are moving until you are confident that you have found a secure place for it. If you have been standing in the same place for some time without moving, check that your feet haven't got stuck without you realizing it.

Always maintain two points of contact with the bottom – either both feet or one foot and your wading staff. When fishing, you will obviously let go of your staff, but then you should keep both feet on the bottom. Go round

boulders rather than over them. Try to use your staff in your upstream hand so that you can lean into the current. If you feel yourself being swept downstream, it is easier to pull yourself towards a well-planted wading stick than it is to push yourself back against the current.

Crossing the Current

When crossing fast-flowing or deep water and you have a companion, cross together with an arm around each other's shoulder or back. The bigger person or strongest wader should be on the upstream side. If there are three of you, put the weakest wader in the middle to provide protection against the full force of the current. Cross the river at a slight angle downstream so that you are not fighting more current than necessary. Do have a good look at the water before venturing in or attempting to cross a heavy run, even if there are two of you together. Try to work out the quickest and easiest route to take. Rapids and deep pool are the places to avoid. River beds strewn with boulders present a real challenge, as it can be all too easy to find your foot trapped in a gap between boulders or to trip over one. If

Below: Always 'fish' your way into a river. Don't simply plunge in, frighten fish close to the bank, and then start casting.

Above: When wading in a stream with a sandy or silty bottom, wade as gently and carefully as you can. If you don't you will stir-up the mud and spoil the fishing for anyone down stream from you.

the going gets tricky, communicate quickly and clearly with your companions and make your way back together.

Reading the water is just as important when wading as it is when fishing. Do take care if you cannot see the bottom, particularly if it was previously visible. If you cannot see the bottom, that may be because you are about to step into a deep hole, so do use your wading staff to keep checking where you are going. It could save you from a soaking or worse. Be conservative and, if in doubt, turn back or get out of the water before disaster strikes.

FISHING AND WADING

On some rivers and streams there will be sections when wading is essential. The banks may be too high or there may be no access on one or both banks. Often heavily tree-lined sections of a river or stream can only ever be fished by wading up the middle. Even on generally accessible rivers, wading can give you an edge when it comes to reaching difficult lies.

Finding Fish

Wading does have the great advantage of keeping your profile lower, particularly when the water is gin clear, but this low profile can make it more difficult to see fish

Above: When wading, it can be helpful to think of the river in strips: one out from the near bank, a second covering the middle and the third from the middle to the far bank. Fish each strip thoroughly before fishing the next one.

at a distance. Sometimes it can be a good plan to spend some time spotting fish from the bank, and memorizing where they are before slipping quietly into the water to make a stealthy approach tucked up against the bank.

Always fish your way into the river. Don't get straight in, as there may be fish close to the bank that you have not seen or, worse, not looked for before getting into the water. If you frighten these fish and they scatter at high speed, they are very likely to frighten other fish over quite a wide area. This is as important in mountain streams, where trout can be made invisible by turbulent water (although they may not frighten other fish for as great a distance as in stiller water), as it is in slow meadow streams with over-hanging, marginal vegetation so loved by trout. Take your time before rushing into a river. Try to make as little noise as possible, and don't let the end of your wading stick bang against rocks. A piece of rubber tube fitted over the bottom end of the stick will reduce the noise.

When fishing in turbulent water you can get surprisingly close to the fish, as they cannot see you so easily

through the air bubbles created by the high flows and rocks. This is, in part, why short-line or Polish nymphing works so well in these rivers. If you wade carefully, you may well be surprised to see fish very close to, or even between, your legs – this is a sign that you are wading very well!

Working Your Way

When wading and fishing the water, it can be helpful to divide the river in front of you into three: a strip along the nearest bank, a strip along the far bank and then the piece up the middle. Fish the nearest strip first before starting to cast over the middle section. Only when you have covered the middle thoroughly should you start to cover the last section. Although you can keep down and out of sight when wading, you will often have to cast very close to, or even right over, a feeding fish, which runs the risk of lining it. If you can, try to change position so that you can cast at an angle, or even ignore the fish in question if, by frightening it, you risk spooking other fish. Sometimes it is possible to wade into a position that avoids having to cast across a section of water with a faster flow that might cause unwanted drag.

If you are wading across the river so that you can get into a better casting position, always do so downstream

Above: Sometimes the first indication of a hatch will be newly-hatched flies crawling up your waders. You should always look to see what flies there are on your waders.

from your target fish, unless you know that you can cross far enough upstream to be out of sight of the fish.

While you are wading, keep looking to see what flies there are on your waders, particularly if there is a hatch taking place. The numbers of flies crawling about, hatching or newly hatched, can be quite amazing. Sometimes the first indication of the beginning of a hatch will be the appearance of a fly on your waders.

Coping With the Down Side

Bear in mind that your field of vision is reduced when wading, making it more difficult to look into the water some distance away from you. In shallow water, say less than knee deep, you can see further than when the water is waist deep.

Once you reach the middle of the river, you will find that you have nowhere to put your rod down when you need to change the fly or the tippet. Unless your vest has a loop and Velcro strap to hold the rod, you will have to tuck it under your arm and then try not to drop it in the river. You will have the same problem when you net a fish, but not if you intend to release one without lifting it from the river.

You'll encounter another disadvantage of wading when a fish rises beyond sensible casting distance upstream. If you simply decide to wade up to it, you risk frightening fish on the way. If you fish your way upstream hoping to catch a fish on the way, the target fish may have stopped rising by the time you get there. The alternative tactics, if possible, are to creep along the edge of the stream, or to get out of the water and make a stealthy approach from the bank. The best course of action will depend on the type of water being fished, together with the number – or lack – of fish in the river.

Below: When changing flies in mid-stream you will have to hold your rod under your arm as there is nowhere to lay it down.

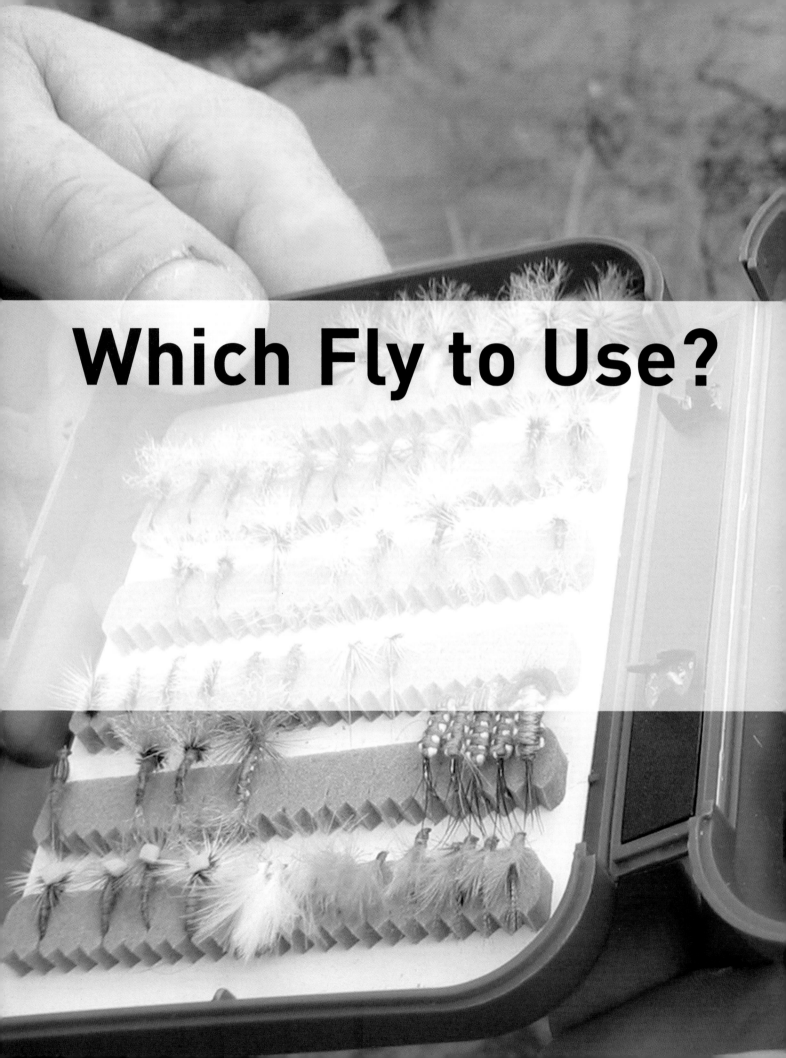

Which Fly to Use?

Which Fly To Use?

When you arrive at the river, your first dilemma will be the right choice of fly. If there is activity at the surface, then the way the fish are rising can provide you with a good deal of information. If there is a hatch underway, you can try to match the hatch, but what is happening on or in the water may demand a more subtle approach than simply emulating the largest flies that you can see. There may be an abundance of more than one species of food item, and you need to know which of them the fish are keyed in to.

Then again, there may be no obvious feeding activity, in which case you'll have to make some educated guesses and experiment a little, but without spooking the fish if you're getting it wrong. A range of searching fly patterns may help you to get on target.

In this chapter we consider all of these scenarios and tactics, as well as the crucial question of presenting your fly in the best way, probably the most important element in fly fishing.

Left: *Watching how a fish is rising is a good indicator of what it might be feeding on.*

Although rise forms are not so easy to see or identify in fast or broken water, there will often be enough of them to give you an idea of what the fish are feeding on, and can help you decide whether to fish a dry fly or a nymph.

General Principles

G.E.M. Skues was one of the first anglers to write about rise forms, nearly 100 year ago. Rise forms show you where the fish are rising or feeding (although not necessarily where they are holding on station), and may indicate what they are feeding on and, to some degree, the enthusiasm with which they are feeding. The rise form and surface disturbance that you see will always be downstream from where the fish actually took the insect.

The size and scale of a rise do not always tell you how big the rising fish is. A big fish taking a nymph just sub-surface may well make a very substantial boil or bulge, but often some of the biggest fish will rise and take a fly with the tiniest of sips, whereas a hungry juvenile may make a major commotion. Quick, splashy rises will often indicate that fish are rising to fast-hatching flies such as caddis or sedges, and in fast water fish have to make a quick decision about whether or not an item – possibly your artificial – is food before it is swept away for ever.

READING THE RISES

A quick scan of a stretch of water may give an angler the impression that everything is straight forward. What can be seen? Flies are drifting gracefully by on their way downstream; fish are rising here and there more or less regularly, sometimes with an audible splash. On goes a dry fly that looks to be a good match of the most obvious flies. After a number of casts with no interest from any fish, our angler begins to wonder what is going on and where he or she has gone wrong.

If our angler takes the time to look more closely and to study the rise forms; these may well show that the situation is not so simple, and may give a good indication of what is actually happening on, in or below the surface.

The Simple Rise

All fly fishermen know the simple basic rise that occurs when a fish floats up in the water, drifting down with the current, to meet the natural or artificial on the surface, which it then takes or refuses. In taking a fly on the surface of the river, a fish's nose and mouth break the surface and produce the familiar concentric rings. If a fish is less than completely confident about the food item that it is considering, it may take time to examine it before taking it or refusing it. A really concerned fish may even turn and pursue the natural or your artificial downstream before taking it. If your artificial should start dragging during this inspection process, the result will be a certain refusal.

The Bulging Rise

A rise form that can be confused with the simple rise is the bulging rise, but the difference is that you will not see any part of the fish breaking the surface. You'll just see a bulge or up-swelling in the water. Bulging fish are taking nymphs or emergers just under the surface. Seeing fish bulging can also indicate that a hatch is about to start, given that the fish are feeding on nymphs high in the water, prior to breaking through the surface film and hatching. A more energetic form of the bulge is a boil, when a fish creates a greater surface disturbance, sometimes with a bit of a splash, too.

The Sipping Rise

Sipping rises are very common in slower-flowing rivers and when fish are feeding on (though not only on) very small mayflies, midge pupae hanging in the surface film, midges or even dead terrestrials trapped in the surface film. Because the food item is barely moving, there is no urgency for a fish to take it. Fish making sipping rises are sometimes said to be smutting.

From the rise form, it is possible to distinguish between surface-feeding cutthroat trout, and other species, such as chub and whitefish, as the latter tend to make bubbles on the water's surface when they rise.

Heads and Tails

One of the most spectacular rise forms is a head and tail rise made by a fish high enough in the water to break the surface. The head will be seen first as the fish takes the fly, probably just under or in the surface film, followed by the dorsal fin and then the tail as the fish heads down again.

Sometimes fish can be seen in relatively shallow water, head down and tail sticking up in the air. Such fish are referred to as tailing fish, and they are grubbing about on the bottom feeding on shrimps, snails and bottom-living nymphs and other insects.

Below: That was a nice meal! A perfect rise to a floating fly. Every dry fly fisherman wants to see plenty of rising fish.

Above: When fishing nymphs it is annoying to get weed on your hook but if the fish are feeding near the bottom, it does confirm that you are fishing deep enough. So always make a point of checking your hook regularly for weed.

Opposite: Two pairs of eyes are always better than one, particularly if one pair belongs to someone who knows the river well. It is also helpful to have somebody with whom to talk about what you see.

NYMPH OR DRY FLY?

Although a sound knowledge of rise forms will help you decide whether to fish with a dry fly or a nymph, if there are no fish to be seen rising and nothing is hatching at the start of a fishing day, it makes sense to start fishing with a nymph, as fish consume 90 per cent of their food below the surface. When fish start moving and flies hatching, you need to be prepared to switch from nymphs to dries and even back again as a hatch progresses and wanes or the fish key in to a different natural or stage of the hatch.

Underwater Action

Of course, if you can identify that the first fish that you see are feeding on nymphs, then that's what you'll go with. Nymphing fish can be seen moving from side to side as well as backwards and forwards, as they turn to intercept nymphs drifting past them. If water clarity is good, look out for the tell-tale flash of white as they open their mouths, as well as any accompanying bulge in the water. When the water is less clear, the rise form may be the main indication of nymphing fish. When fishing a nymph, it is sometimes vital to fish at just the right

depth, even if the pattern that you are using is not absolutely correct. A good match fished at the right depth stands a better chance of success than a perfect match fished too deep or too shallow. It is important to know how deep you are fishing as well as how deep the fish are. Again, it's a matter of close observation, plus experience.

In the Air

Sometimes, before you can actually see flies on the surface of the water, birds such as swifts and swallows may start swooping low over the river, taking flies from the surface and even catching them in the air. To see a swallow take a big mayfly in mid-air is spectacular. You may see these birds flying around quite close to you or further up- or downstream, but their behaviour is a very good indication that flies are hatching and it may be time to think about changing from a nymph to a dry. The hatch may not be close to you, because specific areas on a river will be more agreeable to hatching nymphs than others.

When you can see feeding and rising fish, it pays to try to cast so that you match the fish's feeding rhythm. This is not so easy to achieve when the fish are rising infrequently, but a regular riser will tend to develop a rhythm. Wait for a fish to rise, turn down and swallow its mouthful, and then cast when it will be expecting the next fly to come along. If you are uncertain as to which artificial pattern to use, take the time to look and see where the fish is holding in the water and what it seems to be doing, and use the rise form to decide what it might be feeding on. You may need to change pattern or try a different size of the same pattern.

Below: A fish feeding on nymphs below the surface will often give itself away when it opens its mouth and there is a quick flash of white as it takes a nymph.

MATCH THE HATCH

Some anglers will always endeavour to match the hatch and use an artificial that is the correct imitation of the natural fly on which the fish are thought to be feeding. Some waters do have regular hatches of specific flies at known times of the season – and even at known times of the day – but not many anglers are fortunate enough to fish such rivers. Most of us have to make the best of infrequent or spasmodic hatches, and try to catch fish

Below: A big hairy streamer may not match any hatch, but fished in the right waters they can be very effective, particularly for catching big fish.

that make us feel we are in fly-fishing heaven if they rise more than once or twice in the same place. To be more successful, it helps to spend as much time as you can on them and try to learn when and where hatches and rising fish are most likely to be found. Selecting the right fly can be tricky if more than one species of insect is hatching, and will demand close observation of the water surface.

The Multiple Hatch

When fish start moving and flies hatching, be prepared to switch from nymphs to dries and even back again as a hatch progresses or the fish key onto a different natural or stage of the hatch. Dealing effectively with a multiple hatch is one of fly fishing's more demanding challenges because it is not always immediately apparent precisely which fly the fish are feeding on. When there is a multiple hatch, most anglers tend to represent the biggest fly on the water, as they are the easiest to see and, one assumes, they provide the biggest mouthful for a trout. But fish usually feed on the most numerous naturals, regardless of size, and sometimes the most numerous flies may be tiny.

During a multiple hatch, you must be prepared to change flies when you are not catching fish, and also check the rise forms to see what they can tell you. It can be worth trying an emerger or a stillborn artificial pattern, as either will represent a slower-hatching mouthful for a fish compared to a dun that may fly away too quickly. If this doesn't work, then try a fly of the same pattern but a different size – bigger on fast waters and smaller on slow, clear rivers. On slow water it might be necessary to try a finer tippet as well.

Local Knowledge, Local Ways

When fishing new waters, whether at home or abroad, always be prepared to try the flies that the locals use and recommend. Some of the flies may make a dry fly purist raise an eyebrow in disgust – big streamers, for example – but if you want to catch fish in this new location it may be essential to use such flies, and even to fish them in ways that you have never before considered.

Above: These New Zealand trout are leaving a lake and heading upstream to spawn.

The Yellow-winged Butterfly

The most outrageous fly that I have ever used to catch a trout must be the Yellow-winged Butterfly. It was a fly that I tied during one of the sessions of the fly tying group that used to meet for 12 weeks before and after Christmas. I am sure that there was a good reason for tying such an unlikely-looking pattern – probably learning how to tie with foam.

I was fishing one hot, sunny summer afternoon when a nice fish rose under the far bank. I wasn't sure what it had taken – possibly a damselfly, of which there were a number flying about. I could see the fish in the clear water lying close to the bank. Quite why I chose to have a go at it with the Butterfly I am not too sure. Perhaps I was uncertain that anything would interest this fish, particularly if it had just taken a damsel. Anyway, I tied on the yellow-winged monstrosity. I made sure that the fish was still there, and cast the Butterfly a little way upstream, close in to the bank. The fly floated delicately downstream

looking quite magnificent, just clear of the overhanging bankside vegetation. The fish saw the fly coming, slid to its left and rose higher in the water. It inspected my fly closely, then turned and followed it as it drifted by. Inspection over, the fish liked what it had seen, opened its mouth and made a meal of the outrage. It was never able to return to its lie.

Do fish feel embarrassment?

Above: Peter keeps down on one knee to avoid casting his shadow over the river while waiting for a fish to rise.

FAMILIAR FAVORITES

Like virtually every other angler, I carry boxes full of flies, many of which I never use from one end of the season to the other, but I wouldn't want to be without them. There will always be that one day when one of them proves to be the very fly that I need. I think that I could manage with about seven or eight patterns – both dries and nymphs – in a range of different sizes, but would I want to limit myself to so few? The simple answer is no, although in practice I probably do just that without realizing it. I certainly tend to use the flies in which I have the most confidence.

Pushing the Limits

I spoke to a friend once on the river bank and he asked me if I used the same flies at the beginning of the season as at the end. The question suggests a lack of understanding about the different types of fly that hatch at different times of the year, but the fact is that when you know what you are doing and why, and you fish with a fly or flies in which you have confidence, then you can fish successfully with the same, or very similar, flies throughout much, if not all, of the season. There have always been anglers who insist upon fishing with very few patterns, and there are even some

who take a perverse delight in seeing whether they can manage with only one pattern all season long. This is a remarkable example of total confidence, if not blind faith, but it shows that you can be successful by sticking to your favorite flies. The fewer patterns that you fish with, the less time you will need to spend worrying whether you are using the right fly, but if you do plan to fish with a very limited range of flies, make sure that you have them available in a good range of sizes. Getting the size right can be as crucial as your choice of pattern.

ATTRACTOR PATTERNS

As well as a selection of dry flies and nymphs that will represent known local hatches, anglers should carry some generic attractor flies for those times when there is little or no obvious activity. If there is no hatch to match, you are free from the tyranny of trying to find the right artificial to match the hatch. Whatever fly you put up will have as good a chance of attracting a fish as any other, but a good searching pattern will include a number of key triggers. The more natural flies an attractor resembles, the better the chances are that it will fool a trout into swallowing it. At all times you want your fly to appear and behave as naturally as possible – when you present a fly properly, you can catch fish on flies that don't even attempt to match the hatch. If you can put your fly where and when a fish is expecting to see a food item, you will have a very good chance of catching it, almost regardless of pattern, and possibly size.

Artificial flies should reflect the balance between the selective and opportunistic feeding habits of trout. Ted Fauceglia made an interesting point some years ago in an article in *American Angler* magazine: 'Fly fishermen perpetuate a paradox – we prioritize our flies all wrong. Trout are flesh-eating carnivores; we know this but resist it. Only when the flies we like most to fish – mayflies, caddis flies and terrestrials – don't produce, do we reluctantly resort to patterns that imitate forage foods.' However, if you are specifically targeting large fish, big, bulky streamers can produce great results, particularly at night. Don't be snobbish about fly choices: the best fly is the one that will catch fish.

Productive Tactics

The time to use attractor flies is when there are few fish rising and you want to fish dry rather than sub-surface, but you still need to fish the most likely lies and fish-holding places. Simply fishing all the water is ineffective and will waste valuable time that could have been spent on productive waters. In warm weather or when the water is warm, search out well oxygenated areas and look for springs in the river bed that will provide a flow of cooler and well-oxygenated water. A thermometer can be an invaluable aid to finding springs.

If there are very few or no fish rising, and you do start fishing carefully with an attrcator fly, at least if you get no response you can switch to a nymph knowing that you haven't frightened too many fish. This is easier to do on faster waters, where fish are not able to see as well.

PRESENTATION AND CONFIDENCE

There are two words that should be in the forefront of every fly fisher's mind whenever he or she is on the water: presentation and confidence. Fly fishermen such as Gary Borger have written books on the subject of presentation, and it is undoubtedly the single most important key to successful fly-fishing, particularly for trout. But how can you achieve a successful and consistently high standard of presentation? That's where the second word comes into play – confidence.

Below: Every angler needs a selection of good, generic searching patterns to use when there are no obvious signs of fish feeding, either on the surface or sub-surface.

Above: Even the smartest trout will be fooled by perfect presentation.

Left: If this angler is not very careful, the fish just upstream and in front of him will be under his shadow.

Developing Confidence

Confidence comes with knowledge, practice and experience. You can develop and increase your own confidence by using tackle and flies that you trust and are familiar with. Fishing regularly on the same water and getting to know it well are essential to success. Too many anglers expect success without putting in the necessary time and effort – without serving an apprenticeship, in effect – and they do not understand that they cannot expect to arrive on a river bank and start catching fish straight away. You need to spend time developing and honing your intuitive skills. A good nymph fisherman will develop a sixth sense that tells him when to set the hook – he comes to know that it is the right thing to do at that precise moment. This is not something that you can be taught; it comes by spending time on the water. Try to reduce distractions so that you can concentrate on presentation and effective fishing.

The Art of Presentation

Presentation is not just about casting a dry fly to the right place at the right time. It includes, for example, all the problems of fishing a nymph underwater: casting far enough upstream so that your fly sinks to the right depth, as well as ensuring that it will drift close enough to a nymphing fish to make it want to eat it before it escapes downstream.

Unnecessary false casts risk frightening fish, especially in clear, shallow water, and too many false casts can result in a loss of energy in the fly line that will result in a bad cast. You sometimes see anglers making false cast after false cast, thinking – and hoping – that just one more false cast will see them casting further than they have ever done before and catching that fish under the far bank or away upstream. This is rarely productive. If you do need to make a number of false casts, to dry a fly for example, then try to do so away from the water so that any spray from the line and leader is kept away from feeding fish.

Accuracy, Not Distance

Don't try to cast too far. There will often be fish much closer to you than you might imagine, so don't forget to look for them. Casting too far reduces the accuracy of any cast. Make sure that you look where you want your fly to land, and then make sure to watch where your fly actually touches down. If it's a nymph, you'll see the little splash as it hits and then penetrates the surface. If you can't see where your dry fly has landed and there is a swirl or rise close to where you think it may be, always set the hook. You may not catch a fish every time, but you will be sure to miss fewer this way than if you ignore a potential rise to your fly.

Strategic Casting

Take a few moments to work out and arrive at the best place from which to cast to a fish. You need to think about the angle of your cast, how far away from the fish you will have to be and how long, or short, a cast you will have to make. While you do not want to get so close to a fish that you risk frightening it, there are no medals to be won for making longer casts that necessary. Check the surface of the water for cross or adverse currents that will pull your leader and start your fly dragging. Is there any bankside vegetation that might upset or prevent a good presentation? You may be able to use vegetation to keep out of sight of the fish.

The shadow of your line falling across the water and a feeding fish is something very important to consider when the sun is shining and the water is gin clear, and these factors may determine how you make your presentation. Can you position yourself so the shadow of the line falls away from the fish rather than towards it? This might mean casting from the other bank, or wading across the river. On sunny days, when the sun is high in the sky and behind you, don't forget that your own shadow may well fall across the water and frighten the fish.

Below: If a swirl appears on the surface of the water, or a fish moves near where you think your nymph may be positioned, always set the hook. You may not catch a fish every time, but sometimes you will be rewarded.

Line Control

When fishing nymphs it is particularly important to keep in contact with your fly. It is essential to recover slack line after a cast, and then to retrieve your line at the speed of the river to maintain that contact so that if you do get an offer, you can raise your rod to set the hook. If you have slack line between your rod tip and fly, you will have to raise your rod an exaggerated amount to take up the slack before you can drive the hook home. If a fish takes a nymph it can eject it in a flash if it doesn't like what it feels in its mouth. So being able to react quickly and set the hook before your fly is rejected is vital. Fishing with excessive slack in your line is simply stacking the odds even more in favor of the fish.

That having been said, there will be occasions when you need to keep some slack in your line because too much tension may start your fly dragging sooner than you want; for example, if you have cast over variations in current speed and surface flows. In such a situation, keeping everything nice and taut will cause your fly to drag far sooner than if you fished with some slack in the line. When you do have to fish with a slack line, be prepared to react that much quicker.

When fishing from the bank, it is all too easy to simply drop your fly line on the bank as you retrieve it. You will then undoubtedly find that you have accidentally stood on it, or that it has become wrapped around some vegetation. Standing on a fly line will make it dirty, and you may even damage its surface. Getting your line wrapped round weeds may prevent you from giving line to a fish, or ruin a cast because your line is trapped and won't shoot properly through the rod guides.

There are simple ways to avoid these pitfalls. When retrieving line with your line hand, the speed of retrieve will determine how large you can make the coils of line. If you find that you are making small coils, and you have two coils in your hand, drop one coil as you make the next retrieve. Carry on like this throughout the cast and you will end up with fewer but larger coils. These larger coils will be easier to hold, and they will shoot better as well.

Opposite: *When fishing rough, turbulent water you can get closer to fish than in slower rivers.*

Below: *This angler has the spare line held in neat coils in his line hand, but his line control would be improved by using the fore-finger of his rod hand to hold the line against the rod handle so that he can trap it the instant he needs to set the hook in a fish.*

Streamcraft

Streamcraft

Anglers can't always fish on the best days or at the optimum time, so to make the most of the time on the water it is very important to find the fish and to make the right approach to the water. Streamcraft is about taking the time to observe and think carefully about the likely places to find the fish. Unfortunately not all fish give away their position, so you need to know how to spot fish in the water. It's about working out the best way to execute a well-presented cast that delivers your fly near to where you think the fish is lying so that it will be appreciated by a feeding fish. It's about reaching an individual fish without frightening others and ruining your chances. In short, streamcraft is about thoughtful and productive fishing.

FINDING FEEDING FISH

Fish must eat to stay alive, and they use a certain amount of energy every day simply staying alive. A trout needs to find enough food each and every day to satisfy this basic need. A fish's minimum daily requirement of food – its maintenance requirement – will prevent it from losing weight and condition but will not allow it to gain any weight. How much food is needed to provide a fish with its maintenance requirement depends on a number of factors including water temperature. Even when food is sparse, trout can grow well as long as their food is of good quality, and is available in quantities greater than their basic maintenance requirements.

Influential Factors

In order for fish to feed well, put on weight and live for a reasonable length of time, they require cover from over-head predators, such as herons and other fish-eating birds. They also need to lie in the river out of the full strength of the current, but somewhere that there is a plentiful supply of food that can be eaten with the minimum expenditure of energy. A fish may have a feeding lie as well as a resting one. The first will be where there is plenty to eat, and the second will provide a safe retreat, with protection from predators, where the fish can rest out of the strongest currents and maintain its position with the minimum expenditure of energy. If the current is too strong, too much energy will be wasted staying on station. A plentiful supply of oxygen is also beneficial.

Left: The best fish are usually in the most challenging places, such as close to the fallen branch on the far bank. Structure in a river, such as a fallen branch, will always provide a haven for a fish.

Opposite: A spring creek in high summer. Trout will lie in the gaps between the weed beds where there is a plentiful supply of food, and where they can hide in the weeds when frightened.

The Feeding Lie

If there are no fish rising, the first task is to identify where feeding fish will be lying. A good feeding lie must firstly provide passing food, so it is likely to be where there is a local current or a back eddy, or by a weed bed, rock, boulder or other underwater structure. The tail of a pool, the edge of the main current or a place where two currents meet also create feeding lanes that are hopefully bringing a constant supply of food to waiting fish. Other potential lies include shelves, ledges and drop-offs.

Spring creeks are some of the most challenging fishing situations in the world. Their gin-clear water, slow currents and abundant insects provide ideal habitat for trout. Food lanes are likely to be numerous between weed beds across the width of the river.

Freestone rain-fed rivers and streams experience greater fluctuations in water levels and temperature compared to spring creeks, and water clarity is often not as good. These rivers are likely to have fewer feeding lanes and, indeed, may have only one well-defined feeding lane in a stretch or run, following the main current flow, although bigger rivers will have food lanes where currents diverge and merge.

Above: *The low pressure zone in front of a rock will provide a home for a fish where it does not have to use its energy fighting the current to stay in one place. It will also benefit from a good supply of food.*

Protected Zones

A good feeding lie will also provide, or be close to, protection from predators and will be somewhere the fish can rest out of the strongest currents and maintain its position with the minimum expenditure of energy. The key word here is structure, which means not only rocks and boulders but also tree trunks or branches that have fallen into the river and will provide cover. Look for fish

in front of rocks as well as behind them, as there is always a low pressure area on the upstream side of a boulder or rock.

Surface currents and flows are easy to see, but what happens below the surface is a hidden world to most fishermen. The late Lee Wulff had a good method for testing the speed of flow in a stream using a garden cane with a piece of wool or ribbon tied to one end. He would hold this in the river, just under the surface, and gradually push it down into the river, watching the way the wool flicked and swirled in the flow. Try doing this in front of a rock and you will see that there is a low pressure area, and also that the flow slows as the cane approaches the river bed due to the increase in friction.

Feeding Factors

To be able to catch fish consistently depends on finding feeding fish (or seducing fish that are not feeding actively) and deceiving them into taking an unmissable morsel of food – your fly. The factors that determine

Below: High and low temperatures affect a fish's metabolism, and thus its desire to feed. A fish needs less food when the water is very cold, and if it gets too hot, fish can suffer from oxygen depletion.

whether or not fish are feeding, and how voraciously, include the season, the weather, the water temperature and the level of dissolved oxygen in the water. All of these affect a trout's metabolism and therefore its appetite. Checking the temperature of the water with a thermometer before you start fishing and during the day can provide you with crucial information.

Seasonal Variation

During the winter, when the water is at its coldest, a fish's metabolism is at its lowest, and it needs to eat relatively little to stay alive, but as the days start to lengthen and both air and water temperatures begin to rise, so does a fish's need to feed. Towards the end of winter, snow-melt may cause water temperatures to fall again, but as spring arrives you can expect to find plenty of hungry fish.

As the season progresses, so the amount of food available increases. Although hatches are not often prolific early in the season, they can be triggered by changes in the weather, so if you are fishing on a day when the weather is very changeable you may be able to profit from short but possibly quite intense hatches of flies such as pale wateries and blue-winged olives.

What Food is There?

The thinking angler, or any angler who wants to improve the odds of catching fish, will spend time looking into the river and searching around to find what forms of food are in evidence. At its simplest, pick up rocks or stones and examine what insects and other kinds of aquatic life are either stuck to them or running about when you pick up the stone. A good way to collect nymphs and insects swimming about is with a small seine net. This can be either a landing net with a suitably fine net in the bottom, or you can make your own net with a piece of muslin or fine window netting attached to two pieces of dowel. In either case, the net is placed in the water on or close to the bottom downstream of where you are standing; you then shuffle your feet to stir up the bottom. Anything that is disturbed will be caught in the mesh of the net. A seine net can also be used to catch nymphs and hatched insects near to or on the surface of the water, simply by facing upstream and holding the net in front of you so that it catches anything floating down-stream. The contents of the net can then be examined on the bank. It can be useful to have a white dish or plate to put the bugs on so that you can examine them.

The clarity of a river or stream affects how much light penetrates through the water and, therefore, affects how much and how well trout can see. So when the water is not that clear, or even murky, and there are only a few flies hatching, there is unlikely to be much of a rise.

Top: Using a seine net to find out what food forms there are in a river.
Middle: Making an initial examination of what has been netted.
Bottom: Various cased and uncased caddis larvae found amongst the gravel of the river bed.

Above: *Always make use of bank-side trees and cover for concealment. On sunny days beware of flash from your rod. Always think like a hunter and be as stealthy as possible.*

THINKING LIKE A HUNTER

An experienced, thinking fly fisherman will do all he can to get close enough to a target fish to make a cast of sensible length, but not so close as to frighten it. To have to make a long cast reduces accuracy and increases the amount of line on the water, making the fly subject to more drag. Getting into a reasonably close position will help the angler to make sure that the first cast counts – that the fly lands where the fish is likely to see it and that it looks edible. Obviously there will be many occasions when long casts have to be made, but always aim to position yourself close to the fish. The best position from which to fish can depend on whether fish are rising or if you are fishing the water to find them.

Fishing the Rise

If a fish rises as you approach a river, try to avoid the overwhelming temptation to rush straight up to the bank, or into the water, and cast for it immediately. Pause for a moment and work out the best plan of attack. Time spent observing will never be time wasted, however anxious you are to get fishing and start catching fish. The most obvious place from which to cast may not be the best: your line and leader may have to lie across contrary currents, causing unwanted drag, or the fish may see your line too quickly. If this is the case, you will have to look for, and select, the next best position.

A Bad Example

One summer's day, while I was sitting having a sandwich for lunch, I saw a fellow angler walking downstream towards me along the river bank, stopping and looking, most probably at, rather than into, the water and making the occasional cast. I thought, 'Please keep back from the river or you're going to ruin my fishing.' Later on, when I had started fishing again, he came up behind me to ask how I was getting on. We had a chat and I discovered that he was a relatively new fly fisherman and that, although he had gone fishing several times so far that season, he had never seen a rise, let alone caught a fish. When he had gone, I thought to myself that I was not in the least surprised having seen his attitude and his approach to the river. He was not thinking like a hunter. He would have stood a much better chance of catching fish if he had started at the bottom of the pool – where we met – and worked his way slowly and carefully upstream, stopping every now and then to see what, if anything, was happening.

Seeing Without Being Seen

When stalking fish that you can see clearly, make use of the bankside cover. On open banks keep back from the river when not fishing or when walking up and down. There may well be times (for example, when you cannot get far enough back from the water) when it is better to wade very close in to the bank rather than making a stark silhouette on top of the bank.

There are many factors to take into account when deciding how close to get to a fish and what your angle of approach should be. These include water depth and clarity, bankside cover, the height of the bank, the position of the sun and how heavily the water is fished. The clearer the water, the more important many of these factors become, particularly on sunny days. Take into consideration where you are going to make your false casts in order to prevent rod or line flash frightening a fish. Make sure that you don't stand on the bank waving your rod around aimlessly. If you are turning round, try to do so without casting a shadow over the river with your rod. You may need to change hands or turn so that your back is to the river. Keep your rod away from the water, not pointing over it.

Above: *When the water is shallow and clear and fish can see you easily, get down low and make full use of any cover on the bank, such as this clump of rushes that is just large enough to break up Nigel's silhouette.*

Spooky Fish

A river with plenty of bankside vegetation can be approached much more easily than one in a meadow that is bare. However, fish are rarely frightened by cattle or other livestock on a river bank, and a stretch of water where there are grazing animals might therefore be a good place to try for spooky fish.

On heavily fished catch-and-release rivers, the fish may not be frightened of anglers, but their experience may have taught them to be very wary of flies, particularly if they have been caught and released a number of times. On some rivers, if the fish stopped feeding every time that they sensed or saw an approaching angler, they would soon start to lose weight and condition. In such a situation, although it may be relatively easy to approach such fish, they may scrutinize their food items carefully, and catching them may be another matter altogether, involving pin-point presentation, drag-free drifts and matching the hatch accurately.

Fish will lie sometimes surprisingly tight to the bank. When casting to fish lying close to the far bank of a stream, if your fly does not land on the bankside vegetation every now and then, you are not casting or fishing close enough to the bank. Casting to fish close in to the bank on which you are standing – if not wading – will mean that casts have to be directly upstream and parallel to the bank, or even partly overland with only the end of the line, leader and fly on the water. The problem with such casts is that while they will catch challenging fish, it can be difficult to recover the fly and lift the line off the bank into a new cast, and there's a good chance that you'll get caught up. Freeing your fly from the vegetation may result in the fish you are after being spooked. As long as it doesn't rush off and frighten other fish, it may be a small price to pay, but you can actually benefit from things going wrong.

Every time that you frighten a fish, make a point of trying to see where it goes. Some will simply rush headlong away from whatever has frightened them, but others will go to their hiding areas, and you may be able to use that knowledge later in the day, on another day or

Below: *Big rivers may look intimidating at first glance, but most will have stretches and runs that can be fished as though they are small rivers. Always fish your way into a river: don't just wade out and start fishing, or you will frighten fish near the bank or edge.*

even on another river. Fishing the same or similar waters regularly will help you to build up a picture and store of knowledge of where trout are likely to be found, and this information can then be used when fishing different rivers. All trout have the same requirements, as discussed earlier, although those requirements may be provided in different ways. Your experience can help you decide where to start fishing a new piece of water.

Fishing the Water

When there is no hatch and no fish rising, you can either sit and wait for something to happen, or you can fish the water. This can be made more profitable by fishing the right water rather than simply casting at random. What constitutes the right water can change with time of year, water depth and flow, water temperature and availability of food. Cast to places that provide cover, that give some refuge from the full strength of the current and are adjacent to a food lane. Remember, too, that even on the best of rivers and streams there will be runs that are of less interest to trout, so they will be spread evenly over the length of a river.

Spend time reading the water. Look out for those tricky currents and back eddies that might cause your fly to drag prematurely. Make sure that you have a good approximation of the depth of the water and how deep the fish are holding. Are they close to the bottom? In mid

water? Or just below the surface? While you will want to avoid the currents that will create drag, other currents will bring food to fish, and it's up to you to make these work for you. Look for places that provide shelter for fish out of the full strength of the river's flow – a stone or boulder, a depression in the river bed, patches of weed or weed beds.

Challenging Waters

A smooth-surfaced, gin-clear, gentle stream can be very intimidating for the angler. The harmful effects of every bad cast and presentation will be magnified by the water clarity and the smoothness of the surface. Adding to the difficulty will be those monster trout lurking in the shadows and watching everything that is going on, with a contemptuous sneer on their faces.

Very big rivers, especially fast turbulent ones, can perhaps be more intimidating simply through their sheer size and power, but there is no reason to be over-awed by a big river, assuming that you have the right equipment to fish it. Most big rivers have stretches and runs that can be fished as though they were small(er) rivers in themselves, rivers of a more manageable size, so stand on the bank, look and analyze what you can see. The bigger the river, the more separate, different flows there will be; food lanes, holding lies, resting lies – in fact, many really fishy opportunities.

On some wild mountain or Western rivers and streams it is often worthwhile walking slowly and carefully upstream before starting to fish, to see where the good spots might be and whether you can spot any feeding fish or fish in the water. Water with features or structure is more likely to hold fish than a smooth, featureless stretch. You may not realize that you have passed a good place or fish until you look back and see or hear a rise. If that does happen, retrace your steps, well away from the river, wait for the fish to rise again and then go for it.

Seeing Fish Before They See You

Not all fish are so co-operative that they rise to a floating fly in front of the angler, who can then see where they are. However, when this does happen you need to remember that the rings of the rise were travelling downstream as you watched them, so the fish will be on station further upstream. Also bear in mind that fish often follow flies downstream before rising and taking them, so the fish may be even further upstream than you thought. A well-presented cast that delivers your fly some distance upstream from where you think the fish is lying should be appreciated by a feeding fish.

Below: *Our quarry. A magnificent brown trout in gin clear water.*

Above: *A good way to learn to spot fish is to fish with a friend, taking turns fishing and watching what is happening, and also taking turns guiding each other. When you are fish spotting, get yourself into the best position that you can – here on a high bank – with a good view of the fish being cast to. You will then be able to see how it reacts to each cast and help the caster to place his fly accurately.*

Unfortunately there are more fish that do not give away their position than there are that do. This means that we need to know how to spot fish underwater.

Crystal clear water, a sunny day and a good vantage point on the river bank all make spotting fish that much easier, but they can see you just as easily. Trout are very good at adapting their general coloring to blend in with their surroundings, so you do need to know what you are looking for – even a big fish may not be immediately apparent. Keep your eyes open for something that does not look right or is moving out of sync with, for example, nearby undulating weed. This might well be a fish's tail, which may also be given away by its well-defined, straightish edge that distinguishes it from the soft, rounded shapes of weeds. A fish that is on the fin, in mid-water, and is feeding on nymphs will move about and each time it grabs a nymph it may betray its pres-

ence by a white flash as it opens its mouth or a flash from its flank as it turns.

It is important to practice looking through and into the water, not just at it. Wearing polarized sunglasses eliminates surface glare and makes it much easier to see what is happening under the surface. A high bank that allows you to look down into the river is helpful, as is sunlight, but both factors mean that it is very easy for a fish to see you too. The first thing that tells you there was a fish just in front of you may be the sight of it rushing for cover.

When you are looking for fish, concentration is very important. Even if you think that you are concentrating on looking through and into the water, it is surprising just how many more fish you can see once you start fishing, because now you are really concentrating on what you are doing and you're looking at the river in a different way.

On a sunny day, a real give away of a trout's position can be its shadow on the river bed. On a clean gravel or sandy bottom a fish will cast a dark shadow that can often be easier to see than the fish itself. Even in less than such ideal conditions it is still worth looking for shadows. Use the sun when it is high in the sky to help

you to see into the water, but don't forget that you will cast a strong shadow over the water that may frighten fish. Rough, broken water and pocket water on rivers and streams will help hide an angler from the fish, as it is much harder for a fish to see through the turbulent water.

Partnership

Another good way to learn to spot your quarry is to fish with a friend and take it in turns to cast and to watch what is happening, effectively guiding for each other. This is good fun, as well as being very informative. If, when you are fish spotting, you can get yourself into a good position with an uninterrupted view of the fish being cast to, you will be able to see exactly how it reacts to each cast, and your observations can help the caster to place his fly better. If the fly passes the fish to one side, does the fish show any interest, or is it only interested in flies drifting right in front of it? If using a nymph, is the fly being cast far enough upstream to allow it to sink to the fish's level before it reaches the fish, or is it only getting down deep enough once it's past the fish? Is the fish simply ignoring every cast?

Above: On runs of fast white water (1), use nymphs or wet flies, or fish close in with small dries. In deeper, slower pools (2), use larger patterns, fishing them slowly and allowing them to drift in eddies to draw fish up from 10 to 15 feet down. Steady runs of water three to five feet deep (3) are perfect for dry flies.

Mark That Fish

If you see a fish in the river from the bank and you need to change position or get into the river to cast to it, then you will need to 'mark' its position in the river. This can be easier said than done, as marks or indicators may not work very well from a different position. Keeping this in mind, try to choose marks that you can still see from the new position or, instead of a marker for the fish itself, choose a place from which to cast, and work out how long the cast should be and at what angle. Knowing where the fish is not only improves the accuracy of your casting, but will help when it comes to setting the hook, as you will know roughly when to expect an offer as your fly approaches the right area. Of course, there are fish that will follow your fly downstream and then disappear from view, but at least you'll be ready.

If you find that you cannot see the fish from your new position, even using your marks, just take a minute or two to get used to the new view before making a cast. Look carefully through the water surface in the general area where you expect the fish to be. Study anything that could be a fish very closely. If and when you do spot the fish, you can then cast accurately. If, however, after a thorough search of the area you just can't see anything, then cast to those places where you believe the fish are most likely to be until you either catch or spook the fish.

MATTERS OF STRATEGY

Once you have found the fish and you know that they are feeding, there are still tactical decisions to be made. There may be more than one fish, but can you catch more than one before they all spook? How long should you spend on any given stretch of water before moving on? There may well be obstacles, or weather

Below: When casting to fish lying close to the far bank, if your fly doesn't land on overhanging vegetation every so often you are probably not getting close enough to the bank. A gentle tweak will likely free your fly so that it can drop to the river in imitation of a falling terrestrial.

conditions, that prevent you from making a straight forward cast, so are there any other ways to land your fly in just the right place? These are all questions that should be considered before you ruin your own chances of success.

Which Fish to Catch First?

I once spent a September day on a wonderful stretch of water, and I don't think that I have ever seen so many fish in a river. I ran into a fellow angler and he complained about not being able to catch any fish. He even said he wished the river were stocked. There were shoals of six, eight, ten fish and more, so why would anyone want any more fish? The more I thought about it, the more obvious it was to me why the angler was not catching fish. There were, quite simply, too many fish in the river. The day I fished you could see feeding fish taking nymphs or rising to surface flies, and you could then select which fish you preferred to catch, but unless you looked into the water carefully and thoroughly, you would not see the other fish between you and the one that you wanted to catch. Unless you knew where the other fish were, as soon as you cast to one the chances were that you would line two or three others, frightening off not only them, but the other fish near them as well.

This was a classic lesson in the need for keen observation to identify where the different fish were holding in the water. Once this had been done, it was then possible to cast delicately and accurately to the fish furthest downstream, reasonably secure in the knowledge that there were no other fish between you and it.

If more than one fish can be seen nymphing or rising to duns, choose the one rising most frequently or steadily. Such a fish should be easier to catch than one rising only every now and then. Once again, a little time spent seeing what is happening will bring its rewards.

You can present your fly to more than one fish when fish are lying in a line, but to do this successfully you do need to know that there *is* a line or row of fish. If you succeed in catching the fish nearest to you, get the fish away from the others while you play and net it or you'll ruin your chances of catching the next in line. Try to stop it from rushing up through the other fish, and sending them swimming for cover.

When to Move On

How long should you spend trying to catch a specific fish or fishing in one particular area? It can be all too easy to stay in one place for too long, making cast after cast to a fish that is not feeding or that you may have frightened without realizing it. If you cannot see any fish in a stretch, it may be unproductive, and once you have fished all the water within easy casting range two or

Above: Man-made structures will inevitably attract fish. Fish also lie in the holes made by the flow deflectors sticking out from either bank. They can lie out of the full force of the current, yet plenty of food will be washed down past them.

three times, you should move on.

If you know the river, and you know that fish are few and far between, you may be tempted to spend too long trying to catch a fish that you seemingly cannot frighten. Every river has its wily lunkers, but it is usually better to try new water and undisturbed fish rather than flogging away at the same one.

If you don't know the river and are fishing it for the first time, the temptation is always there to spend too long in one place, but on new water I would recommend fishing fairly fast and keeping on the move – the perfect pool may be round the next bend. If you have time, you can always go back to a specific place and fish it again.

It is better to fish small rivers and streams quite quickly, as there are likely to be fewer and smaller fish-holding areas but, as with everything in life, there will always be exceptions to this. If there is a hatch in progress and you can see fish feeding and rising, then it makes sense to stay in that area, as the hatch may be quite localized.

There are rivers where even the most careful approach and cast will spook fish straight away, and one frightened fish will, inevitably, frighten other fish.

To avoid spooking every fish as you move upstream, you may need to reconsider your approach strategy by, for example, keeping further back from the river, crawling into position to cast, making sure that you are not throwing a shadow over the water – any number of things. While you may end up fishing even more slowly, fishing faster would guarantee that you would frighten even more fish and have virtually no chance of ever catching one.

Resting a fish, pool or run can make a vital contribution to your success rate. Doing this is more difficult for the active angler, and can be a real challenge and test of fortitude. If you think that you have upset a fish or made a heavy, splashy presentation, it is much better to rest that fish or piece of water sooner rather than later. Stop fishing, and back away from the water. Simply carrying on casting is going to upset a fish even more or ruin an even bigger stretch of water. The result will be that you will then have to spend even longer resting the water, waiting for the fish to recover and start feeding again.

Below: *Too many anglers make too many false casts. False casting risks frightening fish, as well as ending up with a bad cast because your rod and line has run out of energy. Here Dave has made a good presentation cast and is allowing the line to run freely through his line hand as he shoots line to ensure he gets the distance that he wants.*

CASTS THAT CATCH FISH

Although the double haul – an additional technique rather than a cast *per se* – is most often associated with lake fishermen who are determined to catch fish as far away from them as possible, for the river angler a short haul of as little as 2 or 3 inches will make a great deal of difference to a cast. It doesn't simply add to the length of the cast; it can also reduce the number of false casts made and facilitate a cast of a reasonable length in confined conditions. A double haul will also help when you are casting into a head wind, as the extra line speed created by the double haul reduces the need for endless false casts.

Reducing False Casts

Rather than giving extra distance, too many false casts cause the rod and line to run out of energy, and your line ends up in an unsightly heap at your feet. If you are a committed false caster, remind yourself to reduce the number of false casts by half every time you cast to a fish. Also, while on the subject of false casts, try not to false cast over a feeding fish, as spray from your line or leader, as well as rod or line flash on a sunny day, may frighten your fish. If you need to extend your line or make a few false casts to dry a fly, try to do this well away from any fish, over the bank if necessary.

Over-long casts risk creating drag and will start dragging sooner than a shorter cast, particularly when cast across variations in current, wind lines and other forms of surface turbulence. As well as being inherently more accurate, a shorter cast will reduce the risk of frightening a fish, or several fish, when a cast gets blown off-course by the wind, or is, quite simply, an awful cast.

Dealing With the Wind

The roll cast is more than just a cast to use when room for a conventional back cast is limited. It can be used to eliminate the back cast if there is a very strong wind behind you. To ensure that you create maximum surface tension when casting a floating line (which is essential to make a good roll cast), do not start the forward roll until the fly line has stopped moving. The resistance provided by the water will ensure that your rod loads properly, and loading your rod properly will ensure a great cast.

Strong winds, especially downstream winds, have always been the bane of anglers, and in the early days of fly fishing it was not possible for the majority of anglers

Above: The off-the-shoulder cast should be used when you have to fish from the 'wrong' bank, or if there is a strong side-wind that might blow your line on to you as you cast. It can also be used to cast round an obstacle.

to cast or fish into the wind. Developments in rod and line technology have changed the situation, but the wind still poses problems. On windy or blustery days there will often be lulls in the wind, so take advantage of these lulls and try to time your casts so that you cast when the wind is less strong.

The wind direction plays a different role when it blows terrestrials onto the water. Depending on the wind direction and whether you are standing on the windward or leeward bank, you may have to cast right into a cross-stream wind in order to land your fly close in to the bank where the terrestrials are landing and the fish are feeding. Taking to the water and wading may be a way of overcoming this problem. A strong wind can also concentrate surface flies – those that have hatched – on one side of a river, pushing them into a feeding lane or blowing them into corners and bends.

A Casting Repertoire

A side-arm cast is used when you need to present your fly under overhanging vegetation or, for example, there is a tree preventing an overhead cast. This is also a good cast to use when you need to keep your rod down to avoid frightening a fish. When you are forced to fish from the 'wrong' bank (i.e. a right-handed angler casting with his line hand closest to the river), or if there is a very strong cross wind use an off-the-shoulder cast. To make this cast, instead of casting with your rod on the same side of your body as your rod hand, you cast with your arm across your body and the rod over your other shoulder. In this way, your rod is next to the water or away from the side the wind is blowing, keeping your line and fly away from your face and eyes.

Another useful cast is the reverse cast, which works very well if trees, for example, grow right down to the edge of the river and you cannot wade out far enough to make room for a normal back cast. To make a reverse cast you need to turn round and face in the opposite direction to that in which you want your cast to go; the forward cast becomes the back cast and the back cast

Below: Not every cast goes according to plan! When you catch your fly on a tree or in bank vegetation, you should initially do absolutely nothing. Do not start tugging and yanking the line. Instead, see if you can find out where your fly is caught, and then see if a gentle pull will free it.

the forward or presentation cast. It is actually much easier than it sounds.

The reach cast will land your fly where you want it, but by moving your rod smoothly to one side or the other just as the line straightens out on the delivery stroke, you will end up with the line well to one side of the fish, thereby allowing your fly to float over the fish well before the line does. The reach cast can also be used to position the fly line away from a strip of faster current flow that might otherwise cause the fly to drag immediately. If you let a little line slip through the rod guides as you make the reach, it will lessen the possibility of pulling your fly away from its target.

Freeing a Tangled Cast

The worst thing that any angler can do when a cast goes astray and does not land where expected – it is hung up on a bush, on a rock, up a tree or caught on bankside vegetation, for example – is to start yanking at it. The first thing to do is nothing. Stop, look to see where your fly is and then decide what to do. If it is caught lightly in bankside vegetation, pull gently on the line itself – not with your rod – and tease the fly free so that it can drop to the water. If all goes well it may even be swallowed by an appreciative and opportunistic fish. Simply pulling hard is most likely to drive the hook further into the vegetation or even break your tippet, and yanking hard with your rod could break it.

When fish are feeding close to the bank – on terrestrials falling into the river, for example – it is often worth deliberately casting a bit too far so that your fly lands on overhanging vegetation, and then tweaking it so that it drops onto the surface of the river, perhaps with the resounding plop that the natural might make. This can be a very effective tactic and should, perhaps, not be in a section on unwanted hook-ups, but it is only by making this mistake that you will come to realize the potential of that cast

If your fly is caught in the stream – on a boulder or rock, for example – a firm upstream roll cast will often free it. A roll cast will pull the fly upstream, in the opposite direction to the way it got caught. If this does not work, it may be necessary to wade up and free your fly or, if fishing from the bank, walk upstream and give your fly line a gentle pull. Pulling on your fly line from a different direction will often do the trick.

On windy days, and when fishing on tree-lined river banks, it is all too easy to end up with your fly up a tree. Again, the worst thing to do is to start pulling on the line, particularly when you cannot reach the end of the branch to pull it within reach. Try the Orvis method of freeing your fly, which works perhaps 19 times out of 20. You need to make sure that you can see where your fly is caught, point your rod up the line and pull the line until rod tip and branch meet. Holding the line tight in your line hand, push the tip of your rod hard against the fly, and then waggle your rod and push up to free it. Some fishermen claim that you risk breaking the tip of your rod or damaging the tip-top, or top ring, if you do this, but this has, so far, never happened to me, and over the years I have succeeded in rescuing a great many flies. The only time that you may fail to retrieve a fly is if it has wrapped itself and a significant length of tippet round a branch. If this is the case, you should continue wiggling anyway, as you may get lucky – the piece of branch just might break off.

Above: Orvis promoted this way of freeing a fly from a tree branch in its catalog some years ago. Make sure that you can see your fly, point your rod up the line and pull the line until rod tip and branch meet. Now hold the line tight and waggle your rod at the same time, pushing up to free your fly. It works almost every time.

Restringing

If you leave your fly up a tree and break your tippet, and you have to restring your rod, the best way to do this is to take the end of the fly line – which you can see easily – and thread that through the rod guides. You will find that this is much easier and quicker than if you were to use the end of the leader, which can be difficult to see in strong sunlight or the gloom of late evening. If your tippet breaks in the middle of a major hatch, you won't want to waste time trying to re-thread your line – you'll want to get right back into action!

Playing and
Landing Fish

Playing and Landing Fish

One of the most exciting sounds that any fly fisherman can hear is the wonderful, electrifying hiss of a taut fly line cutting through the water as a powerful fish makes a run up or down stream. Handle such runs and play the fish well, and you will be rewarded by netting the fish or releasing it while it is still in the water. Get it wrong and everything goes slack, and the best that you can make of it is to say that it was a long-distance release, that wonderful expression that makes something positive out of a disaster.

Above: When you hook a fish and start to play it, it is important to take charge and get it under control as quickly as possible. You may not always be able to follow a lusty fish along the river bank.

KEEPING A LOW PROFILE

Dr J.C. Mottram (1879–1945), who wrote under the pseudonym of Jim Jam, was an English angler who should be very much better known than he is. He was a younger contemporary of G.E.M. Skues, and he wrote a very interesting and thought-provoking book entitled *Fly Fishing, Some New Arts and Mysteries*. Although it was published in 1915, it is still very well worth reading. In his last book, *Thoughts On Angling*, published two years after his death from cancer, he wrote: 'Plunkett Green, in his book, *Where Bright Waters Meet*, repeatedly emphasizes that when playing a large trout on fine gut, the angler must conceal himself from the fish right up to the time when it is ready to be netted.' And then: 'I remember seeing Plunkett Green lay all his long body along a muddy, wet edge of the Test in order to let a big trout go by without being scared.' How many anglers today would go to such lengths, or even consider it necessary to keep out of the sight of the fish that they are playing?

Keep it Calm

It makes absolute sense to do all you can to avoid increasing a fish's sense of panic when playing it. When you think about just how quickly a frightened fish will rush for cover if spooked by a person simply walking along the bank, for example, it is not surprising that if a fish were to see a looming presence when already attached by your fly to a fine tippet, that tippet may not be up to containing a final, desperate break (pun intended) for freedom. Such a loss cannot be passed off as a 'long distance release'. It smacks of bad fishing.

Netting Carefully

Another action that is likely to frighten a fish is showing it your landing net too early. You should have your net ready for action, but try not to wave it around where a fish can see it. Keep it out of the way until you are ready to draw your fish over it, and then lift the net up under the fish. It is wrong to lunge at a fish with a net, trying to catch it or scoop it out of the water. This will cause it to rush off, prolonging the fight or perhaps even breaking the tippet, leaving your fly in its mouth. I once saw a trout swim past me, hotly pursued by what I eventually discovered was a clump of weed caught up in a loop on a length of tippet attached to a hook in the fish's mouth.

As you bring a fish closer to the net, your line is obviously getting shorter and has less shock-absorbing stretch. You also have less time to react and release line when needed, so the chances of a break-off are even greater.

From the moment you start playing a fish, be prepared to net it, as an opportunity may arise sooner than you expect. When fishing from the bank, it is a good idea to have a quick look for a suitable place to net or release a fish. Unhooking and releasing fish in the water is more difficult from a high bank, so try to find a low place, or prepare yourself to slip into the water. When wading, this shouldn't be a problem.

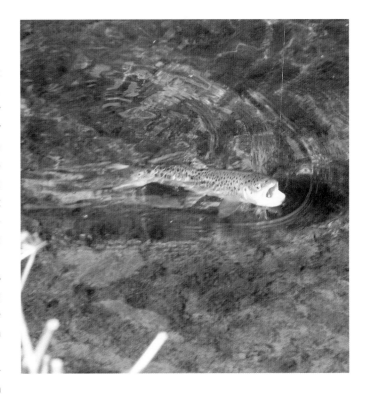

Above: *A fish can often be lost as it makes a final dash for freedom as you attempt to draw it over your landing net. It pays to keep your net hidden until the last minute, and then produce it gently.*

Below: *It is much easier to unhook and release a fish when you are wading.*

CONTROLLING THE FISH

Playing a fish is all about taking control of it and then maintaining that control up to the point when you either net your fish or unhook it. The less time spent playing a fish, the less time is there for something to go wrong. Anyway, no fish that is going to be released should ever be played to the point of exhaustion so that it goes belly up as you bring it in or release it. Fish should be played quickly and efficiently, and netted or brought to hand to be released while still in the water.

Always try to steer a hooked fish away from other fish that you want to try to catch next. A hooked fish rushing around a pool or up and down a stretch of water is highly likely to frighten other fish in the vicinity. Also try to keep in mind where a hooked fish may seek refuge and try to be one step ahead of it, preventing it from making its way round rocks, into thick weed or under submerged branches.

All of this requires you to remain in control of the fish, and that means concentration, skilful use of the rod and the application of just the right amount of pressure.

Below: *This angler has caught a nice trout and is playing the fish on the reel. If you play many fish on the reel, be sure to set the proper drag for your tippet.*

The Upstream Battle

Using your rod correctly will help keep a fish under control and in the area where you want to play it – upstream, so that the fish is fighting the current as well as your line. When you are fishing downstream, or even across and down, you will inevitably end up with a hooked fish downstream from you so that you will have to play the weight of the current as well as the fish. Large trout can be particularly difficult to play downstream, as they often manage to position themselves across the current with their broad, long bodies.

Most people are told to keep the rod tip up when playing a fish, but this is not always the best thing to do. For a rod to act most effectively as a shock absorber, it should be held so that the handle and butt section are at right angles to the fish that you are playing. Changing the angle of rod to the line changes its effective length, and therefore how much pressure you can exert on a fish. Simply holding your rod tip up at all times may reduce the pressure that you can apply on a fish and may simply pull it up to the surface, where it can thrash around and quite probably unhook itself.

While playing a fish with your rod held high and arms extended above your head may look dramatic, if you need to take up slack quickly you'll be unable to do so by raising your arms and rod any further. Keep your arms down and only raise them when absolutely necessary.

Too Much Pressure

In the same way that keeping your rod up is not always the best thing to do, keeping the pressure on and never giving a fish any slack can also be a poor strategy. At its simplest, this is because the more a fish finds itself restrained by the angler's line, the more it will fight to regain its freedom. I once hooked a fish on a nymph on a very slack line and the fish did not start to fight until I actually tightened my line and it realized that it was being restrained. It wasn't worried about being hooked. Giving a fish slack can actually prevent it from heading for an obstruction, such as a weed bed, and a fish in a weed bed will often swim out when you take the pressure off. It's worth remembering that your hook will not fall out of a fish's mouth just because you give it some slack. According to Floyd Franke, in his book *Fish On! A Guide to Playing and Landing Big Fish on a Fly*, giving line to a fish will actually help calm it and stop it fighting against your attempts to keep control of it.

Playing Off the Reel

If you fish for big fish regularly and use a reel with an adjustable drag system, you will need to set it correctly. The drag can be set to simply prevent the spool over-running, or it can be used to apply pressure as a fish attempts to pull line off the spool. Unless you have some experience and are very familiar with your reel, light drag that is enough to prevent over-runs is to be preferred to anything heavier. It is risky to increase the drag during a fight with a powerful fish, as you may increase it so much so that the next time the fish makes a determined run, the tippet is overloaded and breaks. If extra drag is needed, it is better to add it by palming the spool of the reel with your hand.

Hand Lining

Of course, when you are not using your reel but are playing a fish by holding the line in your hand, you will not have this problem. However, playing a fish without using the reel does run the risk of a loop of line snagging on vegetation, or a tangle forming and getting stuck in a rod ring. If you start the fight by holding the line, and then you need to play a fish on the reel, wait until the fish has made a couple of runs before trying to get the slack line onto your reel. Good line management will help when playing fish. Having great loops of line lying on the ground, by your feet or even under a foot, is asking for a snag or tangle to form, perhaps stopping your line from running smoothly through the rod guides when a fish tries to take line from you. Check your line regularly for tangles or knots that may have formed, and remove them straight away.

It is worth remembering that drag increases as you raise the tip of a rod, and as line is stripped from your reel and the diameter of the spool decreases, although this happens less with large arbor reels. Of course, the amount of line that you have in the water also increases the drag.

As was intimated earlier, if you take control quickly and know what you are doing, it is possible, even when fishing with very light tackle, to 'land' a big fish without playing it for so long that the build-up of lactic acid will kill it after it has been released.

Setting the Drag on a Reel

To prevent a reel from over-running, the drag should be set at the lowest point at which this is achieved. Do this by setting the drag at its lightest and then increasing it slowly until you get to the point where a good jerk on the line will make the reel turn, and the line leaves the spool relatively easily but not to excess. To check that you have the drag set correctly, hold the reel in one hand and the line in the other. Pull your hands about 3 feet apart as quickly as you can, without upsetting the reel's function, and stop. If the line between the reel and your other hand is straight, then the drag has been set too tight. If there is a loop of line hanging down more than 12 inches, then the setting is too low.

Above: Fish should be held gently but firmly as you return them to the water.

Anglers in the United States have been strongly encouraged to practice catch and release for over a decade now, and among fly anglers particularly, it has been zealously adopted as something like an ethical philosophy. However, on many rivers anglers do not have the opportunity to make a choice to keep or release a fish. State fish and game agencies across the country use catch and release to manage and protect trout populations, and on many rivers it is illegal to keep a single fish. It is important to learn the regulations for the rivers you plan to fish and to act accordingly. Of course, if you are on a backcountry fishing trip (and the regulations allow it), nothing beats a meal of fresh trout cooked over the campfire.

We have been exhorted to limit our catch, not catch our limit, and this is a good philosophy. It is essential that we all fish sensibly, with due regard for the number and health of fish in a river.

CATCH AND RELEASE

The first designation of a catch and release (C & R) water in the USA was on a stretch of Pennsylvania's Spring Creek, in 1934. Lee Wulff made his famous pronouncement on C & R in 1939 in his book *New Handbook of Freshwater Fishing*: 'Game fish are too valuable to be caught only once.' Then, in 1986, he said: 'Catching trout is a sport. Eating them is not.' His pronouncements are commendable, but bad C & R practices *can* result in the death of more fish than catching and killing your legal limit.

Opposite: An angler is using his reel to bring the fish in to the bank so that he can net it.

Below: This is the sight that every angler who practices catch and release wants to see: a fully-recovered trout heading safely back to its sanctuary.

An Emotional Issue

One of the paradoxes of C & R – and fishing in general – is that anything to do with nature and wildlife, their preservation or destruction, is all too often subject to ignorance and misplaced sentimentality. The C & R 'police' would have every angler believe that this is the only way to fish, and that there are no circumstances under which a fish can ever be killed. This is, of course, complete nonsense. When fishing in the wilderness, with only the limited amount of food that you can take with you by backpack, it may be essential to kill the occasional fish to supplement your diet. When this is done sensibly in, for example, an alpine river that is hardly ever fished, killing a few fish cannot possibly do any harm.

Released to Die?

If catch and release is to be worthwhile, then the needs of the fish need to be taken seriously. There is no kindness or practical benefit to be derived from putting a fish back into the river to die. We have already discussed the need to play fish for as short a time as is reasonably possible. An excessively long and hard struggle can kill a fish, because the rapid use of energy leads to the pro- duction of lactic acid, and leaves the muscles unable to function properly.

The battle also uses up the fish's oxygen. When a fish is netted or brought to hand, its requirement for oxygen is at its highest, so taking it out of the water to unhook it or to take a photograph can cause it to suffocate and die. An exhausted fish should be kept in the water when it needs oxygen most, even if it is a trophy fish that you want to photograph.

Even when a fish is given time and help to recover, and is seen to swim away, this does not mean that it will still be alive 24 hours later. It is a fact that heavily stressed fish that seem to have been released success- fully do not always recover enough to survive. In the summer, when the water is warm, fish take much longer to recover because the water contains lower levels of dissolved oxygen. This means that a fish being played will tire more quickly and it will take longer to recover, as it has to work harder to extract the necessary oxygen from the water. If you do realize that you have released a fish before it has recovered sufficiently to look after itself, quickly catch it by hand or with a net and hold it carefully and gently until it has recovered enough strength to kick itself free from your grip.

Opposite: *When fishing in the wilderness, it may be necessary to kill and eat the occasional fish.*

Below: *It is important to give a fish enough time to recover and regain its strength before releasing it.*

To Net or Not?

There are increasing numbers of anglers who maintain that it is not necessary to use a landing net when fishing C & R waters. They claim to be able to unhook fish in the water without the need to touch or net them. This is certainly true when wading, but not always so easy when fishing from the bank. In theory this must be the best way to release a fish, but what happens when a fish needs reviving? This could mean an exhausted fish being swept away by the current, rather than its captor holding it upright, head into the current, while and until it recovers enough to be able to swim off safely.

Netting fish and then unhooking them does not have to be all bad. It is much easier to hold a fish in a net while you unhook it, but always keep as much of the fish in the water as possible. This helps it to maintain its blood pressure and equilibrium. If you are uncertain about what you are doing, or you lack the confidence to hold a fish while you unhook it, it is better to net it and hold it from the outside.

Handling a Fish

Anytime that you have to hold a fish, make sure that you hold it with wet hands, as this will reduce the amount of

Below: A magnificent wild brown trout about to be returned to freedom where, all being well, it will find a mate and spawn successfully.

protective mucus removed from its scales. Holding fish upside down in the water does help to keep them still. Some fishermen say that when cradling a fish in the water with one hand under its chin while the other holds its tail, it helps to keep a fish still and calm if you put your first finger and thumb in front of its eyes – not touching them, obviously, but close enough to limit its field of view. Gary La Fontaine recommended that when holding a fish, you should avoid touching its lateral line, as it will stay much calmer in your hand. When it is necessary to handle a fish out of the water, hold it firmly; not so hard that you risk damaging internal organs, but firmly enough to avoid the risk of dropping it. The worst thing you can do is to drop a fish on the bank or a rock.

Unhooking a Fish

Some fish that are played quickly and brought to hand to be released will swim off strongly as soon as they are unhooked. This can be done by holding the fly with a pair of forceps, using a Ketchum release tool or even gripping the fly firmly with finger and thumb. Often a lively fish will kick itself free of the fly before you can remove it. If a fly has been taken far into a fish's mouth, making it difficult to remove quickly, it may be better to cut the leader and leave the fly in the fish; this will do less harm than a messy extrication. Some fly tiers recommend tying flies on wide gap hooks as the wider gap makes them easier

to unhook. Such a hook will be easier to grip with a pair of forceps on the bend.

The increasing popularity of barbless hooks and anglers squashing the barb, or de-barbing, hooks does make unhooking and releasing fish quicker and less likely to cause unnecessary damage. Part of this trend is voluntary, and part is the result of compulsion by some state fishing regulations that require the use of barbless hooks only – and often only single hooks. Anglers who fish regularly with barbless or de-barbed hooks do not seem to have problems with losing fish that have become unhooked prematurely, although it may be necessary to keep a little more tension on the line when playing a fish.

Aiding Recovery

The best way to hold a fish in the water is to support its front end under its body and hold it just in front of its tail with the other hand. To help a fish recover, hold it in the current facing upstream and make sure that water is flowing into its mouth and out through its gills. It may help to put a finger in the corner of its mouth to encourage it to open its jaws and let in water. Moving it backwards and forwards will not help it to reduce its oxygen debt and recover.

Support the fish until you feel it starting to try and free itself. When it is ready to go, try not to release it too close to any weed, as it may head for cover in the weed and become entangled.

Above: *Whenever possible it is much better to unhook a fish in the water. But when that is not practical, do it with all speed.*

Below: *When photographing live fish, try not to keep them out of the water any longer than absolutely necessary.*

A Source of Information

Releasing all the fish caught does deny the angler the chance to examine the contents of a fish's stomach to see what it has been feeding on. It is worth having a look in a fish's mouth before you release it – it may be stuffed with food. If do kill a fish, you can learn a great deal by opening the stomach and seeing just what it contains. Items that have been swallowed recently should be identifiable.

Enjoying the River

Enjoying The River

It is a cliché, but there really is more to fishing than just catching fish. For me, fly fishing is one of the best possible ways of getting away from the stresses of everyday life, providing an opportunity both to relax and to enjoy the mental rewards of taking on and overcoming the many challenges that trying to outwit trout and other species of game fish poses.

It offers us a chance to appreciate being on the river, enjoying nature and wildlife and, in some of the more remote places and countries, getting away from civilization completely. Above all, fishing should be a pleasure, but for it to remain so, anglers have a duty to treat their fellow anglers, the natural world and their quarry with respect, behaving responsibly and courteously for the benefit of all and to ensure the future of our sport.

Above: *Ideal fishing conditions. Cool, clear, sparkling water is good for the health and well-being of trout and good for the angler's soul.*

BLENDING IN

A barn owl's white wings are highlighted by the setting sun as it ghosts across the riverside meadows, hunting for mice and voles to feed its young. A flash of electric blue and a piercing call signal the brief appearance of a kingfisher. The observant angler who moves quietly and carefully will see all kinds of wildlife – you just need to know when and where to look. Sitting silently on the river bank or standing immobile and heron-like in the river, it is surprising how close you can get to the wildlife around

you, and this is one of the great privileges of the fly fisher. The river is certainly no place for noisy behaviour.

Bankside Etiquette

The best way to show respect for your fellow angler is to behave quietly and discreetly, and to give him or her room to fish. There are some rivers where two anglers can stand side by side and fish together happily, but in general most anglers would prefer to be left alone with no one else in sight. If you are fishing with a friend then you may well wish to stay close together, but if you are on the river for a day by yourself, that is probably how you want it to be. If there are other anglers on the bank whom you don't know, it is wrong to expect them to welcome you if you start fishing too close to them. If you think that you might be getting too close to another angler, ask if you are. If another angler starts encroaching on your space, politely ask him or her to give you enough room to cast and fish.

The Thoughtful Approach

Casting your shadow across the water when approaching a river or when walking up- or downstream past anglers who are fishing must be avoided at all costs. This is easy enough to do – just look to see where the sun is and keep well back from the edge of the bank if your shadow is likely to fall on the water. Just being on the bank can frighten fish, particularly if it is a high bank. Keep back and keep down. There is nothing more frustrating than working your way slowly, carefully and conscientiously into position to have a shot at the big trout that has been tormenting you all season, when someone suddenly appears on the bank and sends your fish rushing upstream in fear and panic.

Equally, if there is someone sitting watching the river, they may be resting a fish or waiting for it to rise again. Don't assume that the person is not fishing and start casting yourself. Ask first and remember the old maxim: treat others as you would have them treat you. The river bank is still one place where a bit of good old fashioned common courtesy can be expected and given.

When wading across a river, do so well above or, even better, downstream from a fellow angler and out of range of their back cast. When using a bridge upstream of another fishermen, cross the bridge quickly and quietly, and don't loiter looking down into the water for fish. You risk spooking any nearby fish, and you can do that when you are by yourself.

If there is another angler already on the piece of water that you were hoping to fish, approach him carefully, ask if he minds if you start fishing downstream from him or a good distance upstream. He may say that he is just about to move further upstream, or even (best of all!) about to call it a day, so giving the water to you. If he is unpleasant or uncooperative, move on to another location. Rude or aggressive anglers are best avoided. The river bank is not the place for antisocial behaviour.

Enjoyment for All

It would also be nice to think that those who do not fish, but enjoy the countryside and river-side walks, would consider that there may well be people fishing before they throw a stick into the river – followed closely by a large dog! This has happened to me several times, and my loud 'Thank you very much!' is often followed by 'Oh, sorry. I didn't know you were there.' Was I wrong to complain? I don't think so, given that anglers are there to fish while dog walkers are not. It would be a good idea of these walkers took the trouble to see whether anyone is fishing before sending their pets crashing into the river.

Equally, the angler has a duty to check that no one – walker or fellow angler – is nearby before launching into the back cast. A flying hook can do a lot of damage.

Below: Challenging pocket-water fishing in a rocky mountain river. Even in rivers that look like a boiling cauldron, there are lots of places where the current flow is minimal, which provide refuge for fish.

TYPES OF RIVERS

The rivers in the United States can be placed into three categories: freestone rivers, tailwaters and spring creeks. Each of them presents unique challenges that require the angler to adapt and employ his knowledge of streamcraft.

Freestone Rivers

A freestone river is fed by rain, snowmelt and springs. The flow and temperature of these rivers fluctuate throughout the season in relation to the amount of precipitation the area receives. For instance, in early spring a freestone river can be extremely high due to runoff from melting snow, and in the late summer extremely low and warm due to lack of rain.

Freestone rivers range in size from small Appalachian streams to large Western rivers such as the Yellowstone. Other famous freestone rivers include the Gallatin River and the Pere Marquette River in Michigan.

Tailwaters

Tailwaters are rivers that flow out of a reservoir or impoundment. The water released by the dams comes from deep within the lake, and this cool, silt-free water is idea for trout. In fact tailwaters are responsible for creating trout fisheries in regions where there would otherwise not be any trout. Anglers in the South, for instance, can thank tailwaters for the presence of trout in such rivers as the White in Arkansas and the South Holston in Tennessee.

The cool water flowing through the dam allows trout to feed year round. Consequentially, the trout in tailwaters grow to epic proportions. In fact, the world record brown trout – which weighed 40 pounds and 4 ounces – was caught on the Little Red River, which is a part of the White River tailwater system in Arkansas. Double-digit trout can also be caught on the Bighorn River in Montana and the San Juan River in Utah.

Spring Creeks

As the name indicates, spring creeks are formed by water that bubbles up from springs. Spring creeks are intimate bodies of water that are treasured by anglers for their beauty as much as for their high quality of angling. The water in spring creeks is gin-clear and supports abundant insect hatches. Trout grow large and

Left: Freestone rivers range from small to large, and fluctuate from low and slow to high and fast, depending on the season.

Above: Huge fish are often found in cool, silt-free, wide-open tailwaters below dams.

Right: Intimate spring creeks offer anglers wary trout and challenging conditions.

wary in these shallow creeks, and will carefully inspect every insect or fly before biting. Consequently, dry fly fishing for these selective trout is very challenging and very rewarding.

The most famous spring creeks are found in Montana's Paradise Valley: DePuy's, Nelson's, and Armstrong's spring creeks. These three creeks flow through private property and the owners require reservations and charge a fee per angler. However, the experience justifies the expense. Central Pennsylvania has several famous spring creeks as well, of which the LeTort, the Yellow Breeches and Big Spring are most well known.

THREATS TO ANGLING

While there are parts of the world where fishing waters remain virtually untouched and unaffected by human presence, population pressure poses a real threat to many rivers and streams. Many famous Western rivers, for example, have suffered from the over-extraction of water for many years, and the situation is unlikely to improve in the face of demands for even more houses to be built in one of the driest parts of the country. The ever-increasing demand for water will have an increasingly severe effect on the limited water resources, and this problem is not unique to the West.

The Moral Argument

While a shortage of rainfall and increasing demands for water are major concerns in many areas and countries, one of the main threats to the future of angling as a sport comes from changing attitudes. Some problems are self-inflicted, but the anti-fishing activists are getting frighteningly sophisticated in their campaigning tactics, and their messages are being received by a public that is ever more willing to listen to and accept propaganda.

Opposite: Bosse is a Jack Russell terrier and does not always understand the excitement of trout fishing. He is just a happy black and white dog with no appreciation of the niceties of the sport.

Many of those who are against angling believe that it is morally wrong to interfere with nature and nature's ways. What so many of them refuse to understand or accept is that, if it were not for anglers, many, many rivers would have no fish in them today.

Anglers working with such organizations as Trout Unlimited in the USA, and The Wild Trout Trust in the UK spend many happy hours on and in rivers improving them and their habitat to the benefit of fish and flies. Anglers have been concerned about, and have guarded the interests of water ways and the fish in them for many years, reporting pollution incidents, preventing poaching and working to restore rivers damaged by industry.

As Alexander Schwab wrote in his book *Hook, Line and Thinker: Angling & Ethics*, 'Anti-angling is not about fish. It's about what you should think about the world, how you should live and what you should or should not enjoy.' The antis do not want any fly fisherman to enjoy fishing or being on the river.

Although the number of people who are opposed to the idea of people going fishing is growing, in some countries it may not be necessary to ban angling. The sport

Below: The future of angling and wild trout in many countries is under threat due to urban sprawl, pollution, and private developments.

will be ended by ever more urban sprawl, unreasonable demands for water and pollution that will strangle it, slowly at first, but then with increasing haste – death by a thousand cuts.

Every fly fisherman and woman needs to do his or her best to help and encourage the next generation of fly fishers, for today's youngsters are the future of our sport. We must also be on our guard, ready to promote the good that fly fishers do and to counter the often false arguments of those who would deny us our sport. Indeed, who is in a better position to spot a pollution incident and report it to the authorities than an angler on the river?

A Sporting Attitude

Anglers who mishandle fish, leave live fish flapping on the bank or attempt to kill one with a stone or a piece of wood deserve the ire of their fellow anglers. Abusing fish is playing into the hands of the antifishing lobby, as it confirms for them that angling is a cruel sport. If you are going to kill a fish, do it quickly and with the proper tool. For many of us, the days of killing any fish are long past, and the enlightened fishing magazines and websites now rarely use photos of dead fish. Photographs like those of 19th Century anglers triumphantly display-

ing vast bags of dead fish will never been seen again, thanks in part to the practice of catch and release, but mostly because, with rare exceptions, there simply are not the same numbers of fish in the rivers today.

It has been said that every would-be angler wants to catch a fish, that he or she then wants to catch every fish they possibly can, and then they want to catch the biggest fish. Sadly, there is some truth in this and, worse still, some anglers never get past the stage of wanting to catch the largest number of fish that they can every time they go fishing. Others are only happy when they can catch a big fish, even if that means a genetically manipulated, pellet-fed monster. This is not the way to protect the future of fishing.

Anglers need to understand, promote and practice sporting values, hard though this may sometimes be. Fly fishers should look forward to catching a small number of challenging fish rather than ever greater numbers of fish. If these are all wild fish, so much the better. A little moderation and self-control never did anyone any harm. This is a philosophy and practice that may take time to develop, but there needs to be an appreciation of the difference between catching a few high-quality wild fish and bagging dozens of stocked fish, and an understanding that fewer really is better.

Below: *When you have caught a fish as fine as this, what is there left to do? Just enjoy the moment.*

Opposite: *Anglers should be satisfied catching small numbers of fish in challenging conditions.*

CONSERVATION

In certain regions of the world, rivers are coming under increasing pressure based on the various demands being made upon them. As may be expected, the pressure being placed upon these rivers is threatening the fish living within them. Examples of strain being put on these rivers include the over-abstraction of water for drinking and for irrigating farmland; run-off from roads and silt from fields filtering into the water; and pollution incidents such as factory emissions or leaks and the spillage of toxins into waterways. Thankfully, help is at hand from organizations such as Trout Unlimited (TU) and the Federation of Fly Fishers (FFF). Both organizations do exemplary work in helping to preserve and enhance fish habitats. Advice on river restoration and habitat improvement is available from these organizations (see page 140 for contact details).

Below: *A nice stretch of small-stream wild trout water. The bankside trees will provide overhead cover for fish, and will also act as a source of food items, such as caterpillars.*

River Protection

Many rivers that flow through farmland suffer from low, slow flows and a build-up of silt. One solution to this problem is to reduce the width of the channel in certain places. Bank narrowing of over-wide stretches can help to speed current flow, and to remove silt. Different techniques can be used to reduce the width of a river channel, including staking and tying in place bundles of wood to form a new river bank; this 'bank' can then be back-filled with gravel. Emergent and riparian aquatic vegetation will soon colonize the new river banks.

Other threats to fish stocks include poaching and over-grazing of bank-side vegetation. One quick and easy way to prevent the over-grazing is to fence off the banks. Enclosures can be fenced off on the outside of bends, and then planted with trees which will provide shelter and fly life. Cattle drinks can be provided as necessary; if these are filled with large stones for the cattle to walk on, this will help reduce the amount of silt that might otherwise find its way into the river.

Increasing the Population

Making gravel riffles will provide increased variety of habitat, extensive areas of well-oxygenated water and some challenging fishing. This is work that requires heavy machinery and many tonnes of stone. Works of this scale are far beyond the scope of most anglers or those concerned about the state of our rivers, as the cost will be substantial. But if the funds can be raised and the materials and machinery assembled, the results could be dramatic. Fish will often take-up residence on new riffles within hours of their installation. Furthermore, fish that stay on new riffles will provide sport in areas in which they might not have been caught before.

Another way to increase fish population is to encourage spawning. One way of encouraging wild fish to spawn is to make sure that you have areas of clean gravel with a good flow of water. Potential spawning gravels can be cleaned and freed from excess silt by using water-jetting equipment; this consists of a water pump and a hose with a metal pipe on the end, which is then forced into the gravel. The water pressure then washes away the silt, leaving behind clean gravel.

Above: *There is much that can be done to restore and enhance trout habitat, as here, where a gravel riffle has been made. The riffle will help put oxygen into the water, and it will also provide a gravel bottom for spawning trout.*

Below: *Clean, silt-free gravel is essential if trout are to spawn, and thus maintain a healthy population of wild fish. Managing a fishery to ensure that it has good spawning areas is hard work, but it is also enjoyable and rewarding.*

Fishing Further Afield

Fishing Further Afield

A fishing trip to new waters is an opportunity to learn new methods, to find and fish with new patterns of fly and to catch different fish. Many more anglers are traveling and experiencing the thrill of a new challenge. Planning carefully what you are taking with you – especially clothing and equipment – and packing everything sensibly can make a huge difference to your enjoyment, particularly if your adventure involves airline travel. However, the most important factor will be the attitude you take with you. An open mind is vital, as is a willingness to use local flies and listen to advice. In many places, the rules and regulations that govern your home waters may be radically different. You can fish upstream, downstream, down and across, use wet flies, streamers and anything else that your conscience and pride will allow you to use. Make the most of the opportunity.

RESEARCH AND PLANNING

Before making a booking for a fishing trip, do plenty of research so that you are sure that the fishing is going to be the sort that you want to do, and that the rivers and streams suit your style of fishing and your level of experience. If you do not like to wade, a remote hike-in river is probably not suited to you. You will probably have more pleasure on a nice spring creek or a meadow river. There are rivers that can provide a good range of different conditions, or it may be a good idea to go to a part of the world where you can fish on several different rivers that offer a range of fishing styles, perhaps starting on something small and gentle before working your way up to more serious wading conditions.

Below: Many rivers that are home to trout and other game fish are surrounded by beautiful scenery. Travel gives the angler an opportunity to fish different types of waters, and to experience and enjoy new landscapes.

Rods and Tackle

Depending on where you are going, the types of rivers to be fished and the size of fish you hope to catch, you may want to take a heavier line weight rod with you. A 5-weight, nine-foot four-piece is a good all-rounder, but some people prefer to use a 6-weight. If at all possible, do take a spare rod with you, in case of a breakage. You may well be many miles from a fishing tackle shop, and if you break your only rod, that may be the end of your fishing. If you are going to be out in the wilderness, it pays to be self-reliant. Having said that, a friend who broke his rod when fishing some back-country rivers in New Zealand was able to arrange a replacement free of charge under the terms of the maker's guarantee.

It is also well worth investing in a quality reel with a good drag and the capacity for plenty of backing, as you may well see your backing for perhaps the first time. Big fish in powerful rivers can take some controlling, particularly if you get rainbow downstream from you. You may need to be able to give line to a fish as you negotiate rapids or climb over and around rocks on the river bank.

Below: When fishing rivers that are located well away from civilization, it is always a good idea to be as self-reliant as possible. Take a spare rod with you, just in case.

Above: Travelling by floatplane to reach your destination will afford great views of the countryside below, but they do have limited luggage capacity, so think hard about what you want to bring along on your trip.

Opposite: Pocket waters will demand a new approach for any angler used to fishing only lowland rivers. There are more suitable lies for fish in these rocky, turbulent rivers than seem possible.

Hidden Costs

Between hotels, fishing licenses and replacing whatever gear you inevitably forgot at home, the cost of a fishing trip can quickly add up. There are many ways to control expenses on a trip: you can camp instead of booking a hotel, rent an economy car rather than an SUV, and bring plenty of extra leaders, tippets and other supplies. Another way to cut your expenses is to buy your flies in bulk before your trip. This can save you as much as 20 cents per fly which, when you are buying dozens and dozens of flies, quickly adds up.

Airplane Travel

Eventually you will want to travel to some far flung river across the country or around the world, and for this you'll need to travel by airplane. The rules regarding carry on luggage, tackle and other equipment are always changing, so be sure to get the most current information from your airline prior to booking your trip. Here are a couple points to keep in mind when traveling by airplane or floatplane:

You will be limited to the airline's restrictions on the size and weight of your luggage, so pack only what you need and leave the rest at home.

Lost luggage is a fact of traveling, but you can hedge your risk in the event the airline loses your luggage by spreading your gear among all your bags. For instance, don't put all of your reels or flies in a single bag; divide them among all your luggage.

Check with your airline on what tackle and gear they allow in your carry-on luggage. Most allow you to bring your rods onboard, but double check this before departure, and carry on whatever is permitted.

If you will travel via a floatplane to your final destination, check with the lodge or outfitter about weight restrictions for your gear.

Travel Tips

• Take a simple tool kit with you so that you can carry out essential repairs, particularly if you will be a long way from a tackle shop. A good multi-tool will probably suffice, but do make sure before you go that your screwdriver blades will fit any screws on a reel that may need tightening or unscrewing. A roll of duct tape or similarly strong tape can be used to fix a loose rod guide and many other items.

• Try to be prepared for the unexpected. You may encounter freezing temperatures in the mountains in mid-summer, or you might be expected to eat or drink an exotic local speciality. It's all part of the fun of fishing foreign waters.

• A tube of suncure wader repair, which cures using UV light, will repair holes in waders very quickly so valuable fishing time won't be lost.

• A good fixed blade or pocket knife is likely to prove invaluable for everything from preparing and eating food to cutting wood for a fire (this should be packed in your 'checked' luggage).

• A length of cord or a thin line will work as a replacement lace for a wading boot, as well as tying luggage together.

• Heavy-duty plastic bags can be vital if it rains and you need to keep spare clothing dry. Use them as well for packing wet or dirty clothes for the trip home.

• A bottle of whisky will help make friends in most fly-fishing locations, and can be enjoyed as part of a celebration after catching a trophy fish.

Mosquitoes!

Concerns about mosquitoes figure high on the list of those going fishing in the Alaska, New England, Canada and other areas where these wretched insects thrive. If you are susceptible to mosquito bites, as I am, be sure to go well prepared. Take the most powerful insect repellent that you can find – look for a high level of Deet – and be prepared to use it regularly. If you don't like the idea of smothering your face in insect repellent, then take a bug net. Ideally, do both. A mosquito net has the advantage of keeping flies and insects off your face and head and out of your mouth, and you can even sleep in one if necessary.

Mosquito bites can be very unpleasant, as I found out to my detriment some years ago. The weather was variable, and the mosquitoes came and went as the weather changed. There were days when there were hardly any mosquitoes about, but they were very aggressive when in evidence. I was bitten on one side of my mouth during the evening, and when I woke up the next morning I could hardly speak or see out of one eye, as the whole of one side of my face had blown up. Fortunately I had plenty of antihistamine tablets and cream to stop the itching, and everything was back to normal within a few days, but it was not an enjoyable experience at the time and my companions were very concerned, as we were several hours away from civilization. So be warned. If you are well prepared, mosquitoes can still be a nuisance, but a bearable one, so don't be put off going to the far north.

Sensible Clothing

As well as using a bug net or repellent, keep as much of your skin covered as possible. For example, wear a long-sleeved polo-neck sweater under your shirt and keep the shirt cuffs buttoned up. If you need to roll up your sleeves to cool off, don't forget to apply repellent to your bare arms. Make sure that any hat you wear has no breather holes in it, or block them up before you start your trip. If it has holes, our friends will pass through them and start feasting on your head.

Don't wait until you reach the river to start taking precautions. Make sure you have your insect repellent to hand, and apply it as you leave the airport. There may not be as many mosquitoes here as there will be on the river, but you only need a few bites for the wretched itching to start.

Opposite: *Taking the time to sit quietly and enjoy awe-inspiring scenery is one of the best parts of the fishing experience.*

Below: *When fishing in the wilderness it is sometimes necessary to kill fish in order to eat it – trout, pickerel, or the best, fresh salmon. Nothing tastes quite like a fish cooked over an open fire and eaten within a few minutes of its capture.*

Above: Not much compares to the peace and tranquillity found in Alaska, where one can fish and not see another soul for miles.

Left: The correct choice of footwear for wilderness fishing is very important: you should have footwear that will perform just as well in the river as on dry land.

Hiking and Wading

The right choice of footwear is important, especially if you are going to be hiking into the river, or doing a lot of walking to and from the river and up and down the banks. Felt-soled wading boots are great in the water, but they are not as good on dry land. Hiking-boot-style wading boots are available, but it is also worth considering taking a pair of lightweight hiking boots that you can wear instead of wading boots. This way you will save your expensive wading boots, and you'll have something comfortable to wear for any serious hiking that you may have to do.

GUIDED FISHING

While it certainly makes sense to listen to what your guides advise about the best times and places to fish, don't let them dominate your thinking. During the course of one trip we experienced very hot, sunny weather, and the guide said that we would never catch anything during the day: the only time to fish was through the night. We did as we were told, but two of us also fished during the day, and we both caught some super fish – big rainbow and brown trout – and had a great time. Our success was not very well received, but I had confidence in what I was doing (as well as wanting to prove the guides wrong!). I have never worried too much about fishing on hot sunny days. I know that it is not always easy, but I also know that you won't catch fish unless you are fishing. Much of the fishing that I do is between about midday and 2pm, give or take an hour, and whenever I'm asked what is the best time to fish, that is my answer.

Following Advice

In some instances, however, it really does pay to listen to your guide. For example, I was told some years ago by a local guide in Montana that if you want to catch rainbow trout, fish a goldhead nymph, and if you want to catch brown trout, use something big and bushy. This was good advice, and it certainly worked. I caught some of the biggest browns I have ever caught on a version of a Woolly Bugger fished down and across, stripped fast to imitate a large hatching caddis on its way to the surface. The bow waves that followed my fly before these monster fish hit it had to be seen to be believed, particularly in the deeper parts of pools just before the rapids – very exciting!

Below: *Fishing a river from a drift boat with a guide provides a new and exciting experience for many anglers. This will be one time that you will need to heed your guide's advice.*

Above: *Staying at a lodge is a good option for those who prefer to have their meals ready and waiting for them after a hard day's fishing on the river. Some lodges will also provide boats, equipment and guides upon request.*

Opposite: *Camping allows the angler to get off the beaten track and head for more remote areas. However, it is crucial that you do not neglect safety considerations in these circumstances, particularly if you are camping alone, or staying out for some time. Make sure that friends or family and any local wardens or rangers know of your intended location, transport arrangements, and when you intend to return. Check with the local authorities what regulations, if any, exist regarding the lighting of fires. If you do light a fire, make absolutely certain that you put it out completely when leaving it unattended. Make sure you have reliable communication equipment – mobile phones often lose their signals in remote areas.*

Choosing Accommodation

Fishing trips can involve staying in a lodge or floating down a river in an inflatable boat. If you plan on floating a river, stopping and fishing the good spots on the way, you will have to take your own food and provisions with you. When staying in a lodge, however, one can expect to be fed well (hopefully meal times will be flexible enough to accommodate the angler's known propensity to ignore food when the fishing is hot!), and for there to be a well-stocked bar. In northern latitudes, when it is light throughout the night, you will want to have the opportunity to fish around the clock. A well-organized lodge should be able to provide meals at a time that will suit those anglers about to fish the night shift, as well as accommodating those anglers who prefer to fish during the day. Little can compare with a freshly cooked hamburger and a beer at six o'clock in the morning after a great night's fishing. And there is nothing worse than worrying about getting back to a lodge before the kitchen closes for the night, perhaps as the best rise of the day is getting underway.

More robust souls may decide that they want complete flexibility and go for a self-catering camping holiday. Camping can be great fun when the weather is good, but it is inevitably less pleasant if it is wet and you are stuck with wet gear that needs drying out, or if your tent leaks. If it is really wet and cold outside, you can always live in your chest waders and wading jacket. This is perhaps not the most hygenic of options, but you will probably stay dry! It's all part of the fun and adventure of going on a fishing trip.

WHERE TO FISH

One of the greatest joys in fly-fishing is to explore new waters. A new river is like a puzzle but, with your new knowledge of streamcraft, one you will be able to solve. Fortunately, the Unites States is blessed with an abundant variety of rivers, which I have divided into three categories based on geography: The West, The Rest, and Alaska. Should you ever become bored with North America, however, there is always our neighbor to the south.

The West

The western states of Montana, Wyoming and Idaho contain, arguably, the best trout rivers in the world. Nowhere else in the world has as much diversity and selection as these three states.

In Montana anglers will find the Madison River, which is renowned for its regular and prolific hatches, such as the Mothers' Day Caddis hatch in mid-May, and the Salmonfly hatch in late June. These hatches draw thousands of fish to the surface, and the dryfly fishing is extraordinary.

Just a couple mountain valleys to the east of the Madison flows the majestic Yellowstone River. This wild freestone river is the longest undammed river in the

Below: Alaska offers spectacular fly fishing opportunities for both trout and salmon.

lower 48 states. The most popular stretches flow through Paradise Valley south of Livingston, Montana.

Straddling the border of Wyoming and Montana, is the fly-fishing Shangrila known as Yellowstone National Park. This 3,470 square mile park contains a lifetime's worth of small streams that flow out of the surrounding mountains and through achingly beautiful valleys. Slough Creek, the Fire Hole and Soda Butte Creek draw most of the anglers, but there are scores of lesser known creeks and rivers to be discovered in the backcountry – if you are willing to hike through grizzly bear country.

The Henry's Fork of the Snake River near Island Park, Idaho, is known for its excellent dryfly fishing. The selective rainbow trout here can test the mettle of even the finest anglers. But just across the border in Jackson Hole, Wyoming, anglers target the eager cutthroat trout (a relative of rainbow trout) that live in the South Fork of the Snake River.

The Rest

The rest of the Lower 48 states contains a broad selection of rivers of all types and sizes. Starting on the West Coast, anglers can fish for trout on the Upper Sacramento River in California, and on the coastal rivers of Washington and Oregon, anglers chase large rainbow trout known as "steelhead."

Colorado holds many excellent rivers that rise out

of the Rocky Mountains. The Roaring Fork River near the mountain town of Aspen flows past huge mansions and lush golf courses before joining the Colorado River. The nearby Frying Pan River is also worth a visit. The Au Sable River in northern Michigan is famous for its brown trout and a hatch of giant mayflies in the early summer.

East Coast anglers head to the Delaware River system in central New York for the wild trout that live there. In fact, the Catskills region of New York is considered to be the birthplace of American fly-fishing. In Arkansas, the White River tailwater system produces fish that are measured in pounds rather than inches. Night fishing for these double-digit brown trout is an exhilarating experience.

Alaska

Alaska has long attracted anglers to its wild lands. With much of the land uninhabited and undeveloped, Alaska comes as close to fishing in a true wilderness as can be found in the 21st century. Bristol Bay is a sure bet for catching large rainbows that grow fat by feeding on the eggs of Pacific salmon. In fact, Pacific salmon are an excellent flyrod quarry if you can get one to bite your fly. King salmon up to 50 pounds are not unheard of on a fly rod. Anglers who want to experience the Alaskan backcountry can take multi-day float trips down rivers such as the Nushagak, where you are more likely to encounter a grizzly bear than another angler.

South America

In Argentina, the Rio Caleufu starts its life in the foothills of the Andes, then it meanders through forests and rolling hills. There are plenty of hard-fighting wild browns and rainbows to be caught on streamers fished from drift boats. Access to the lower reaches is much easier than to the upper river. Anglers looking for a quiet spring creek might consider the Arroyo Pescado, which flows through a treeless valley in the province of Chubut. This is not to be confused with the Chilean river with a similar name.

Chile must be one of the very best destinations for the travelling trout fisherman. The country has wonderful fishing, fantastic scenery, food and wine and charming people. The Futaleufu is a big, gin-clear freestone river that can be floated as well as fished from the bank. It divides into channels, which are usually easier to fish than the bigger turquoise waters. Rain can be a problem, but rivers with lakes on their course are usually fishable after heavy rain.

Below: Every angler wants to catch a trophy-size trout. There's no one best place to catch them, but Montana is without a doubt a great place to try.

Some Essential Flies

Some Essential Flies

Every fly fisherman tries to put together a small universal selection of flies that will catch fish anywhere and in every season. There are, indeed, certain dry flies, nymphs and streamers that will produce fish in a wide range of water and conditions, and every fly box should contain most of these in different sizes, as well as a range of generic patterns that can imitate many naturals when the right size is fished. Alongside a good basic selection of artificials, you will undoubtedly want to add your own regional specialities and personal favorites to this list, but in this chapter we look at dressings for some of the most universally popular flies.

DRY FLIES

CDC and Elk

Hook: Tiemco 102Y, 11 to 18 (or equivalent dry fly hook)
Thread: Brown 6/0
Body/hackle: CDC feather
Wing/head: Fine tipped deer hair, well marked with a light body and black tip

The CDC and Elk was developed by the well-known Dutch fly tier Hans Weilenmann during the 1992 season. The design soon established itself as his number one general purpose surface pattern. The fly was inspired by Al Troth's Elk Hair Caddis (see opposite). All the materials in the pattern contribute to its great floatability, and it is surprisingly durable.

Gray Wulff

Hook: Partridge down-eye,10 to 24
Thread: Grey
Tail: Natural bucktail fibres
Body: Muskrat or grey squirrel fur
Wing: Brown barred squirrel-tail hair
Hackle: Two blue dun and one dark red cock hackle

The Gray Wullf is one of a series of hair-wing patterns designed in the 1930s by the late Lee Wulff, who wanted a buoyant fly that represented a good meal for a big, hungry trout. This fly has become one of the most popular mayfly (*E. danica*) representations in the US. Although many commercially tied flies have their wings pointing forwards, this was not Wulff's intention; they should in fact stand vertically.

Adams

Hook: Dry fly, 10 to 22
Thread: Black or grey 8/0
Tail: Brown and grizzly hackle fibers
Body: Muskrat or medium grey dubbing
Wing: Grizzly hackle tips, tied upright and divided
Hackle: Brown and grizzly mixed

The Adams was invented in 1922 by Leonard Halladay, of Michigan, and it is now one of America's most successful and popular dry flies. Halladay designed it to represent a deer fly on the Boardman River. It is an invaluable general pattern and, while it has spawned many variations, the original is still an essential pattern in any dry fly box.

Humpy

Hook: Dry fly, 10 to 18
Thread: Black, red, yellow or green
Tail: Moose or elk body hair
Body: Tying thread or floss
Overbody: Moose or elk hair
Wing: Tips of moose or elk hair over body, upright and divided
Hackle: Black or brown, or brown and grizzly mixed

The Humpy is a very durable buoyant pattern, particularly when fished on fast, rough water. It is an excellent attractor pattern that can be said to represent anything that a trout wants to eat. It is accepted that the name 'Humpy' derives from the humped body, but just who invented it is uncertain. It may originate from near Jackson Hole, Wyoming, or from a fly tier in San Francisco.

Elk Hair Caddis

Hook: Mustad 94840 or TMC 5210, 6 to 24
Thread: Tan, olive or black, 6/0 or 8/0
Rib: Fine gold or brass wire
Body: Tan, olive or black Antron
Hackle: Brown, furnace, grey or black, palmered
Wing: Natural tan elk hair
Head: Clipped elk hair

The Elk Hair Caddis was designed by Al Troth of Dillon, Montana, in the 1970s, and can be tied in a wide range of sizes and colours. It is very versatile as it can be used as a searching pattern, as a stonefly in large sizes, as a caddis or stonefly in smaller sizes and even as a midge in very small sizes. When tied in different shades – dark and light – it can be fished to match the hatch, but when used as a searching pattern it is best tied in an easily visible colour.

Klinkhåmer Special

Hook: Partridge GRS15ST, 8 to 18
Thread: Uni-Thread 8/0, grey or tan for body. Spiderweb for parachute hackle
Body: Fly Rite Extra Fine Poly dubbing for normal or large flies, Wapsi Super Fine Waterproof Dry Fly Dubbing, color to suit, tied very slim
Wing: Wapsi white poly yarn, one to three strands depending on size of hook and water to be fished, or siliconized yarn for small flies
Thorax: Three strands of peacock herl
Hackle: Blue dun, dark dun, light dun, chestnut, all in good color combinations with body

Hans van Klinken, another Dutchman, developed this fly in the early to mid 1990s. He was inspired by the well-known Swedish fly, the Rackelhanen, and he first used a Klinkhåmer Special, a sub-surface hanging parachute pattern, fishing for grayling on the Glomma River in Norway. He always stresses the importance of tying his pattern on the correct hooks with the correct choice of top-quality materials.

'F' Fly

Hook: Dry fly, 12 to 18
Thread: Black 6/0 except for size 18 hook 8/0, or any dark color such as red, olive, green or brown
Body: Tying thread, tied slim
Hackle: One to three CDC feathers, according to hook size, natural colors or dyed pink for grayling

Marjan Fratnik, a Slovenian, produced his famous fly as an improvement on a CDC pattern tied by a tackle shop owner in Basel, Switzerland. Marjan wanted a fly that was more visible than the original, and also more durable. He fishes it tied on size 14 hooks, with natural color feathers, except in difficult light conditions when he uses yellow or orange CDC feathers for better visibility.

Tying Tips

Very small flies can benefit from being tied on wide gap hooks, as they will hook and hold more securely. For anyone with less than perfect eyesight, it will make your life much easier if you buy flies tied on hooks with over-sized eyes, or you can tie your own flies on this kind of hook. Threader fly boxes that can be loaded at home in good light are another way of making it simpler to attach a fly to the end of the tippet when you are at the river.

Parachute Adams

Hook: Dry fly, 10 to 22
Thread: Grey
Wing post: White calf tail or poly yarn
Tail: Grizzly hackle fibres
Body: Adams Grey Antron or Superfine dubbing
Hackle: Grizzly

A British patent was granted to the American William Avery Bush in August, 1932 for the design of the parachute hackle.

CDC Bubble-wing Emerger

Hook: Dry fly, 8 to 22
Thread: Fine, color of choice
Tail: 2 or 3 strands of pearl Kyrstalflash
Body: Tying thread
Wing: CDC feathers tied in as a bubble

CDC feathers can be used to make very effective generic emerger patterns, and there are many tying variations available. The key points to imitate are the trailing shuck and the protruding, hatching wings.

TYING THE 'F' FLY

Marjan Fratnik's 'F' fly was first publicized in the Slovenian fly fishing magazine *Ribic* in 1983, and then in an article the following year in the German magazine *Fliegenfischen*, written by Marjan himself.

He has fished for over 70 years, not just in Slovenia but all over the world. He now fishes 'F' flies almost exclusively, mostly tied on size 14 hooks tied with natural color croupions or CDC feathers. If light conditions are difficult, he uses yellow, orange or white flies. If a fish refuses his fly after a number of presentations, he will pull it underwater just in front of the fish.

The 'F' fly is a very simple fly, as it is tied with only tying thread and between one and three croupions, depending on the size of hook: 12, 14, 16 or 18. Thread color can be black or other dark colors such as red, olive, green or brown. Tie a very slim body – Marjan uses size six thread, except for size 18 hooks where he uses size eight – and then take the appropriate number of feathers - one or two for small hooks, three or four for the largest. Pinch them together with your fingers, with the ends even, and cut the thick ends neatly with sharp scissors before tying them on top of the hook shank. Complete the head with a neat whip finish. The other end of the feathers can be trimmed to length, directly over the bend of the hook for slow rivers and chalk streams, and an eighth of an inch longer for faster rivers. Cut them on the long side rather than too short. The head can be finished with a drop of varnish. The 'F' fly: simple to tie and effective to fish.

NYMPHS

Gold-Ribbed Hare's Ear Nymph

Hook: 2X long nymph, 10 to 16
Thread: Black 6/0
Weight: Lead wire

Tail: Hare's mask guard hairs
Body: Hare's mask dubbing
Rib: Fine gold wire or oval gold tinsel
Abdomen: Hare's mask dubbing
Wing case: Mallard wing quill segment tied over thorax
Thorax: Hare's mask dubbing, well picked out

The origins of this fly are 'lost in the mists of time', although in its dry form it was one of the best patterns fished on the Test and Itchen in the middle and latter years of the 19th century. Some authorities claim that the Hare's Ear could be 500 years old. Whatever its age and origins, it is still a supreme artificial either in its original nymph form or with the addition of a gold, copper or black bead head.

Sawyer Pheasant Tail Nymph

Hook: Down eye Limerick, 14 to 20
Tying thread and weight: Fine red-colored copper wire or UTC Ultra Wire SM Copper Brown

Tails: Tips of four center fibers from a browny-red cock pheasant tail feather
Body: As tails
Thorax: As tails

Frank Sawyer, who was a river keeper on the Wiltshire Avon, based the design of his most famous nymph on a well-chewed Pheasant Tail Red Spinner, his favorite dry fly. He was the first person to dispense with tying thread and to tie a fly using only fine wire as both tying thread and ballast. It remains unsurpassed as a representative of olive nymphs when tied in different sizes. It can be fished at different depths, depending on how much of the tippet is greased.

Bead Head Gold-Ribbed Hare's Ear Nymph

Hook: 2X long nymph, 10 to 16
Thread: Black 6/0

Weight: Lead wire
Bead: Gold, copper or black
Tail: Hare's mask guard hairs
Body: Hare's mask dubbing
Rib: Fine gold wire or oval gold tinsel
Abdomen: Hare's mask dubbing
Wing case: Mallard wing quill segment tied over thorax
Thorax: Hare's mask dubbing, well picked out

Bead Head Sawyer Pheasant Tail Nymph

Hook: Down eye Limerick, 14 to 20
Tying thread and weight: Fine red-color copper wire or UTC Ultra Wire SM Copper Brown
Bead: Copper or gold
Tails: Tips of four center fibers from a browny-red cock pheasant tail feather
Body: As tails
Thorax: As tails

Copper John

Hook: TMC 5262 or equivalent, 12 to 22
Thread: Black 6/0 Danville or Ultra Thread
Bead: Gold or brass

Weight: Lead wire
Tail: Brown goose biots
Abdomen: Wapsi copper Ultra Wire, or color of choice
Thorax: Peacock herl
Wing case: Thin Skin, pearl Flashabou and epoxy
Legs: Hungarian partridge or hen back or saddle

The Copper John was designed by John Barr of Boulder, Colorado, who tied it with copper wire. Since about 1996, it has proved to be a very popular and successful nymph imitation, and it is now tied in a range of different colors. As it is quite a heavily weighted, quick-sinking pattern, correlate the size of Copper John to be fished with the depth of water: deep water, big flies; shallow water, small flies.

Prince Nymph

Hook: TMC 3761, 8 to 16
Thread: Black 6/0 or 8/0
Tail: Brown turkey biots
Rib: Flat gold tinsel
Body: Peacock herl
Hackle: Brown hen hackle
Wings: White turkey biots

This nymph was the creation of Don and Dick Olson of Bemidji, Minnesota, and it was named after Doug Prince of Monterey, California, who popularized it.

Grey Goose

Hook: Down eye Limerick, 16 to 20
Tying thread and weight: Fine gold wire
Tails: Herls from the primary wing feather of a farmyard grey goose
Body: As tails
Thorax: As tails

This is another of Frank Sawyer's nymphs, tied to represent lighter colored naturals.

STREAMERS

Olive Woolly Bugger

Hook: Down eye 3X or 4X long, 6 to 12
Thread: Black 6/0 or 8/0
Bead: Brass, gold or tungsten, optional
Weight: Lead wire
Tail: Olive marabou, with 6 to 8 strands of olive Krystalflash, optional
Rib: Fine copper wire
Body: Olive chenille
Hackle: Olive or black hen or soft cock hackle, palmered

The Woolly Bugger is tied to imitate small bait fish such as minnows or even leeches. It is not the most polite nor the most gentle pattern, but, nonetheless, it is very effective in the right conditions. It was first tied by Russell Blessing of Lancaster, Pennsylvania, in 1967, when he added a marabou tail to a Woolly Worm to imitate a hellgrammite. His original pattern had a peacock herl body and black ostrich tail. The modern version is cheaper to tie and more durable. It can be tied in a range of different colors and color combinations.

Black-and-Orange Marabou

Hook: Mustad #9672, Nos. 2-10
Thread: White flat waxed nylon
Body: Gold or silver flat Mylar tinsel, medium
Rib: Gold or silver oval Mylar tinsel, medium
Wing: Black and orange marabou
Head: Black head cement
Eyes: White or yellow with black pupils

An excellent streamer that imitates a variety of minnow species, the Black-and-Orange Marabou is an excellent pattern to use when fishing new rivers. Quick strips will create the impression of a fleeing minnow that trout find impossible to resist.

Mickey Finn

Hook: Mustad #9575, Nos. 2-10
Thread: White flat waxed nylon
Body: Silver flat tinsel, medium to wide
Rib: Silver oval tinsel, medium to large
Wing: Top-yellow dyed bucktail; middle-red or crimson dyed bucktail; bottom-yellow dyed bucktail
Head: Black head cement

The Mickey Finn is a streamer pattern that dates back to the 1930s. It is a classic and for good reason – it catches fish. However, it has fallen out of favor with the current generation of fly anglers who seem to fish the newest and gaudiest streamers rather than the old standbys. Do not make that mistake – this fly will catch everything from brook trout to rainbow trout in a variety of conditions.

Marabou Wing Black Ghost

Hook: Mustad #9575, Nos. 2-10
Thread: White flat waxed nylon
Tail: Yellow calftail
Body: Black yarn, 2- or 4-ply
Rib: Silver flat Mylar tinsel, medium
Throat: Yellow calftail
Wing: White turkey marabou
Head: Black head cement; painted eyes optional

The classic Black Ghost was first tied in the Rangeley Lakes region of Maine in the early 1930s for brook trout and landlocked salmon. However, I prefer the addition of a marabou wing rather than the original feather wing. Although it hails from New England, this fly will catch fish from coast to coast.

Above: *Although trout find most of their food subsurface in the form of nymphs, pupae and shrimps, it is a fish's rise to a fly floating on the surface of a river that every dry fly angler craves, and that makes his or her heart miss a beat. The Mayfly (E Danica) is one of the largest of the upwing flies.*

Left: *Caddis flies are most often seen at rest away from the water atop vegetation. Trout will feed on them frenetically both as pupae and as emerging adults. Caddis flies have a four-stage life — egg, larva, pupa and adult. (Upwing fly life is also comprised of four stages: egg, nymph, sub-imago (dun) and imago (spinner)). Caddis flies have tent-shaped wings and no tails, whereas upwing flies, true to their name, have wings that are carried upright, and can have two or three tails.*

Fly Tying on the River

The late G.E.M. Skues would often get up early and, before breakfast, tie a selection of flies for the day ahead. He also had a small fly-tying vise with a semi-circular plate that he held between his teeth so that he could tie flies on the river bank, with the aid of a magnifying glass clamped into his one good eye. Oliver Kite was another angler who always had a small selection of fly tying tools and materials with him, carried in the trunk of his car when he went fishing. Skues' tying ability with his mouth vise must have been challenged, as his flies were much more complicated to tie than Kite's simple nymphs, such as his bare hook nymph and the pheasant tail nymph.

I once saw a beautifully designed and intricately crafted antique finger vise, fashioned from brass, with bronze jaws that were opened and closed by a screwed, knurled round 'nut' that ran up and down a threaded shaft. A clip held the vise on one finger while you held the hook and the jaws of the vise with your index finger and thumb.

Special portable vises have been available for many years, and they are still made today. Some are designed to be used in one hand, while others come with attachments so that they can be fixed onto the branch of a tree or a fence post. But how many anglers these days take the time and trouble to assemble a small, universal fly tying kit and carry it with them, so that they can tie a fly to match the hatch or tie some replacements for the killer pattern of the day? It would be a great tradition to revive, as it really reflects the true spirit of fly fishing.

Practical Knots

Practical Knots

Knots are the potential weak link between the angler and his or her quarry, unless the right ones are used and tied correctly. Some knots are too complicated to tie under pressure on the river bank, surrounded by rising fish and with the light fading fast, but there's a simple knot for almost every situation you're likely to encounter. Once your backing has been attached to the reel (using the arbor knot) and your fly line is joined to the backing (with either a nail knot or an Albright knot), they can be forgotten about for most of the season. The knots that you'll be tying on a regular basis are those used for attaching the tippet to the end of your leader and the fly to the end of the tippet. Always choose knots that you can tie quickly, easily and correctly, and that experience has shown won't slip or break under extreme pressure. Use knots in which you have confidence, and try not to make things any more complicated than necessary. This is one area of fly fishing that benefits from keeping things simple.

Arbor Knot

You know you're into a good fish if you get to the end of your backing, but it can happen, and if that knot gives way you'll lose a lot more than just the fish. Tied correctly, the arbor knot won't let you down.

Begin by passing the tag end of the backing line around the reel spool, or arbor, between the spool and the reel foot. Tie an overhand knot around the running line **(Step 1)** followed by a second overhand knot at the tag end of the backing **(Step 2)**. Work the first knot close to the arbor, before trying to tighten it. To tighten the knot, hold the reel in one hand and pull on the backing line with the other **(Step 3)**. The knot in the tag end acts as a stopper for the second knot.

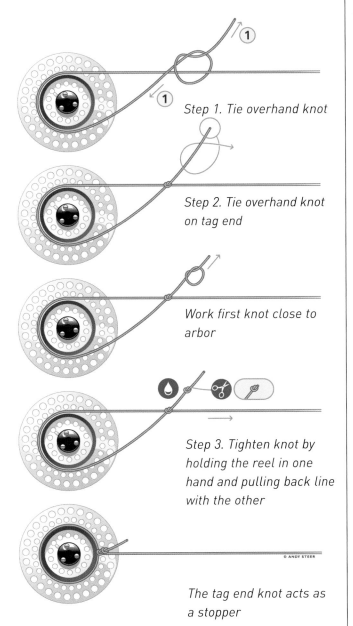

Step 1. Tie overhand knot

Step 2. Tie overhand knot on tag end

Work first knot close to arbor

Step 3. Tighten knot by holding the reel in one hand and pulling back line with the other

The tag end knot acts as a stopper

Trilene Knot

The great benefit of using this knot to attach flies is that the tippet goes through the eye of the hook twice, producing a much stronger knot. For very small hooks, where the eye is too small to thread the tippet through twice, you will have to use another knot such as the improved clinch knot (see page 137).

Thread the end of the tippet through the eye of the hook from underneath and then through a second time **(Step 1)**. Hold the fly with your finger and thumb and keep the double loop open, having adjusted it for size. The smaller the loops, the easier it is to tighten the knot. Wrap the tag end of the tippet around the standing part five or six times **(Step 2)** and then pass the tag end through the first loops that you made **(Step 3)**. Moisten the knot and tighten it by pulling the tag end and standing part together or alternately **(Step 4)**.

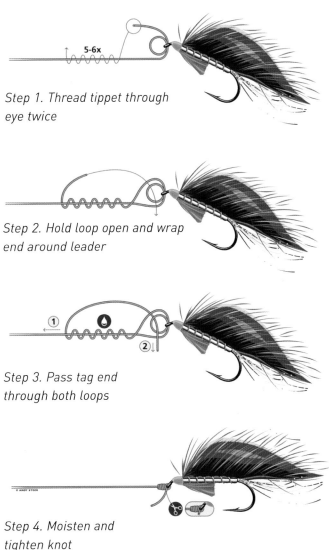

Step 1. Thread tippet through eye twice

Step 2. Hold loop open and wrap end around leader

Step 3. Pass tag end through both loops

Step 4. Moisten and tighten knot

Albright Knot

The Albright knot is one of the best for joining two lines of different diameters or materials, so it is also suitable for attaching the backing to the fly line.

Make a loop in the end of the thicker of the two lines to be joined and hold it with your finger and thumb **(Step 1)**. Pass the tag end of the other line through the loop. Pinch this tag end against the other lines and wrap it round all three strands, from left to right **(Step 2)**. Make at least 10 wraps and ensure the wraps touch each other **(Step 3)**. Pass the tag end of the thin line through the loop so that it comes out on the opposite side of the loop it first went through **(Step 4)**. Still holding the standing part of the thick line with your left hand, pull the standing part of the light line at the same time as working the wraps towards the end of the loop. When the wraps are tight against the end of the loop, pull the tag end of the lighter line really tight with a pair of pliers. Check that the knot is tight by pulling on the standing parts of both lines **(Step 5)**.

Step 1. Make loop in end of thick line

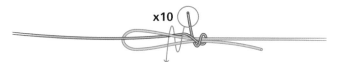

Step 2. Wrap thin line around thick line

Step 3. Make at least 12 touching wraps

Step 4. Pass thin line through loop

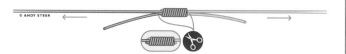

Step 5. Work wraps to end of loop
and tighten knot

Surgeon's Knot

This very efficient knot is quick and easy to tie. It is excellent for joining pieces of mono (for example, adding a tippet to the end of the leader).

Lay the tag ends of both lines alongside each other, ends together. Take hold of both lines and make a large loop **(Step 1)**. Pass the ends of the lines through the loop, making an overhand knot **(Step 2)**. Repeat this step again **(Step 3)**. Hold the standing lines and the tag ends, moisten the knot and pull it tight by pulling all four ends at the same time **(Step 4)**. Before trimming the knot, pull the individual lines to make sure that it is fully tightened.

Step 1. Make large loop with both lines

Step 2. Make overhand knot with both lines

Step 3. Make second overhand knot

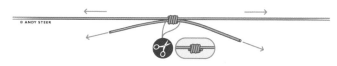

Step 4. Moisten and tighten knot

Leader to Fly Line

There are various ways to attach the end of a non-braided leader to the fly line, including braided loops, making a loop in the end of the fly line as suggested earlier or attaching a length of heavy mono of the appropriate thickness and stiffness. The thick end of a braided leader can be threaded over the end of the fly line and then glued in place..

Improved Clinch Knot

This is probably the knot used most often for attaching flies to the end of the leader. The simple clinch knot is not as secure – the final tuck of the improved version makes all the difference.

Thread the end of the tippet through the eye of the hook from underneath **(Step 1)**. Hold the hook and both pieces of the tippet with your finger and thumb and as you start to wrap the tag end round the standing end of the tippet **(Step 2)**. Make sure that you hold open the loop formed by the first wrap. Make at least four wraps before passing the tag end through the loop that you are keeping open with your thumb and finger **(Step 3)**. Now pass the tag end back through the loop that you have just made. Moisten the knot with saliva and tighten it by holding the hook and pulling the standing end of the tippet, not the short tag end **(Step 4)**. Pulling the tag end can ruin the knot.

Some people tie this knot by holding together the standing part and the tag end of the tippet and twisting the fly to make the required number of wraps, but this method results in the loop immediately in front of the eye of the hook being very small, making it that much more difficult to pass the tag end through it, particularly in poor light conditions.

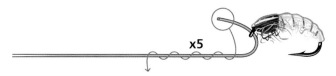

Step 1. Thread tippet through hook eye

Step 2: Wrap tag end around leader

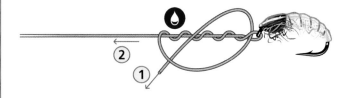

Step 3: Pass tag end through loop

Step 4. Moisten and tighten knot

How Many Wraps?

When tying an improved clinch knot or a Trilene knot, the number of wraps you'll need to make with the short tag end will depend on the thickness of the line. Too few turns of thin monofilament may result in the knot slipping, and too many turns of thick monofilament may be too difficult to tighten correctly and fully. With tippets of between 3lbs and 5lbs breaking strain, you should, as a rule, make at least four or five wraps.

Nail or Tube Knot

This knot is ideal for connecting the fly line to the backing, or a leader to the fly line. As its name suggests, to tie this knot you need a nail or a short piece of thin tube.

Lay the tag end of the fly line against the nail or tube, with the standing part of the line to the left and the tag end to the right. Now place the butt end of the leader (or backing) against the tube and line, but pointing in the opposite direction **(Step 1)**. You need about 10 inches of the leader to tie this knot. Hold the fly line, leader and tube or nail firmly in your left hand. Wrap the tag end of the leader around from left to right in touching turns **(Step 2)**. Use the finger and thumb of your left hand to stop the wraps from separating or unravelling. When you have completed six or eight wraps, insert the tag end of the leader into the right-hand end of the tube **(Step 3)**. (If using a nail, slide the nail out and feed the leader through the tunnel left by the nail.) Change hands and, taking care not to let anything slip, pull the tag end of the leader through the tube, or tunnel, with your left hand.

Now you need to remove the nail or tube, keeping firm pressure on the knot with your right hand **(Step 4)**. Now pull the tag end of the leader so that the wraps start to tighten on the fly line. As you do this, slide the wraps towards the end of the line, to position the knot. Pull on the standing part and tag end at the same time to tighten and seat the knot **(Step 5)**. Trim the tag end of the leader close to the knot and also the end of the fly line if the knot isn't close enough to the end.

Step 1. Lay ends of tubes alongside nail or tube

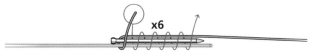

Step 2. Wrap tag end of leader around lines and nail

Step 3. Make six to eight wraps

Step 4. Remove nail and pass line through gap

Step 5. Tighten wraps and knot

Tie Your Own Knots

Once you have learned to tie your favourite knots, never trust anyone else's knots – always tie your own. All anglers have their preferred knots and types of tippet materials, and so you may not get the knot that you need, which is why allowing a fellow angler to tie a knot for you is often a guaranteed way of losing that fish of a lifetime.

Surgeon's Loop

The use of a surgeon's loop on the end of the leader and on the end of the tippet is the quickest and easiest way to join the two, using the loop-to-loop connection. The surgeon's loop is tied in the same way as the surgeon's knot (see page 136), but it uses only one length of mono.

Make a loop with the tag end of the leader or tippet **(Step 1)**, hold it with your left hand and tie the loop in an overhand knot **(Step 2)**. Pass the end of the double line through the loop a second time **(Step 3)**. Moisten the knot and tighten it by holding the tag end and the standing line together in one hand, passing something that will not damage the line through the loop and then pulling. Trim off the tag end to complete the knot **(Step 4)**.

Step 1. Make loop in end of line

Step 2. Tie loop in overhand knot

Step 3. And a second time

Step 4. Tighten knot and trim tag end

Tidy Knots

Always trim the tag end of a knot carefully and as short as possible. Little stubs left sticking out will inevitably catch small pieces of weed and ruin your presentation.

Loop-to-Loop Connection

Once you have two lengths of line or monofilament with a loop at one end of each, pass the loop on the end of the standing line through the loop on the line to be connected **(Step 1)**. Now pass the end of the line to be connected through the loop on the end of the standing line **(Step 2)**. Pull all of the line through the loop to tighten the connection **(Step 3)**. Pull both lines so that the two loops interlock to form a square knot that will distribute the stress evenly and equally **(Step 4)**. This is how the finished connection should look when tight. The connection can be undone easily should you wish to change tippets.

Step 1. Pass standing line loop through other loop

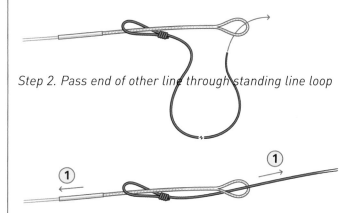

Step 2. Pass end of other line through standing line loop

Step 3. Pull line through loop to tighten

Step 4. Pull both lines so that loops interlock

The Knot or the Line?

If you lose a fish and leave your fly in its jaws, take a close look at the end of your tippet. If it is tightly curled like a pig's tail, then chances are that the knot slipped, but if it is clean and straight, your tippet most likely broke.

CONVERSION FORMULAE

To Convert	Multiply by
Inches to Centimeters	2.540
Feet to Meters	0.3048
Yards to Meters	0.9144
Miles to Kilometers	1.60934
Ounces to Grams	28.3495
Pounds to Grams	453.592
Celsius to Farenheit	1.8 and add 32

FURTHER READING

John Bailey, *Improve Your Fly Fishing* (New Holland, 2003).

John Bailey, *John Bailey's Complete Guide to Fishing* (New Holland, 2001).

Floyd Franke, *Fish On! A Guide to Playing and Landing Big Fish on a Fly* (The Derrydale Press, 2003).

Tom Fuller, *Getting Started in Fly Fishing* (Ragged Mountain Press, 2004).

Ed Jaworowski, *The Cast* (Swan Hill Press, 1994).

Mel Krieger, *The Essence of Flycasting* (Club Pacific, 1987).

Tom McNally, *The Complete Book of Fly Fishing, 2nd Edition* (Ragged Mountain Press, 1993).

Dr J.C. Mottram, *Fly-fishing: Some New Arts and Mysteries* (The Flyfisher's Classic Library, 1994).

Dr J.C. Mottram, *Thoughts On Angling* (Hebert Jenkins Limited, 1945).

H. Plunkett-Greene, *Where The Bright Waters Meet* (Modern Fishing Classics, 1983).

Charles Ritz, *A Fly Fisher's Life* (Max Reinhardt, 1959).

George V. Roberts, *Master the Cast* (Ragged Mountain Press, 2002).

Frank Sawyer, *Keeper of the Stream: The Life of a River and its Trout Fishery* (George Allen & Unwin, 1985).

Lee Wulff, *Lee Wulff on Flies* (Stackpole Books, 1980).

Lee Wulff, *Trout On A Fly* (Nick Lyons Books, 1986).

CONTACT INFORMATION

Federation of Fly Fishers
215 E. Lewis Street,
Livingston, MT 59047
Tel: 406-222-9369
www.fedflyfishers.org

Trout Unlimited
1300 North 17th St., Suite 500
Arlington, VA 22209
www.tu.org

INDEX

Page numbers in *italics* refer to illustrations

ACKNOWLEDGMENTS

My thanks go to Bill Dod and Peter Whiting for arranging two very good, enjoyable and different days on the river Kennet, and to Nigel Rich for organising access to some exclusive rivers in Norfolk and Derbyshire, and to Peter, Nigel, Dave Pitchers and Jérome Philipon for their co-operation and allowing me to photograph them when fishing. Thanks also to Spencer Johnson, for tying some of the flies illustrated in the book. Ulf Börjesson, John Bailey, James Andersson, Bill Dod, Martin Ede, John Klingberg, Richard Nelson and Mark Williams all allowed me to use one or more of their photographs, for which I am very grateful. Many thanks to everyone at New Holland Publishers, and finally, many thanks to my wife, Ingalill, for taking my dog for walks when I am away fishing.

PHOTOGRAPHIC CREDITS

All photographs taken by Terry Lawton, with the exception of the following, which are © John Bailey: p10-11, 16(b), 27, 37, 40, 41(t), 56, 57(b), 59(t), 62, 64, 77, 86, 92, 99, 100, 101, 105, 107(b), 114, 115, 116(b), 118, 120. Page 129(tr, bl, br) by Jim Dugan.